Lieutenant
Heinrich Carl Philipp von Feilitzsch
and
Lieutenant
Christian Friedrich Bartholomai

Diaries of two Ansbach Jaegers

Translated and Edited
by
Bruce E. Burgoyne

Other Heritage Books from Bruce Burgoyne

Waldeck Soldiers of the American Revolutionary War
A Hessian Officer's Diary of the American Revolutionary War
Eighteenth Century America
Georg Pausch's Journal and Reports of the Campaign in America
Enemy Views: The American Revolutionary War as Recorded by the Hessian Participants

Published 1997 by

HERITAGE BOOKS, INC.
1540E Pointer Ridge Place
Bowie, Maryland 20716
1-800-398-7709

ISBN 0-7884-0655-8

Table of Contents

Preface....................v

Introduction....................ix

Map of New York/New Jersey area....................xii

Diary of Lieutenant Heinrich Carl Philipp von Feilitzsch....................1

Map of Charleston, South Carolina area....................85/86

Diary of Lieutenant Christian Friedrich Bartholomai....................86

Notes....................156

Index....................163

Preface

The first contingent of Hesse-Cassel troops which sailed to America in 1776 as auxiliaries to help England suppress the revolt in the American colonies, included one company of jaegers, or as the term translates into English, hunters. The second contingent, which arrived later the same year, also included one company. Each company had a strength of four officers and 125 men.[1]

Dressed in their hunter-green uniforms, the men, who were trained in forestry crafts and were excellent marksmen, proved themselves to be very proficient in combatting the 'American Indian' style of fighting employed by the colonists and England sent Colonel William Faucitt, who had been the negotiator of the first treaties for hiring the "Hessians", back to the continent to engage as many more of these foresters as he could. In a special treaty of December 1777, Hesse-Cassel agreed to increase the jaeger commitment from 260 to 1,066 men.[2]

A treaty with Ansbach-Bayreuth in 1777 initially provided for two infantry regiments and one jaeger company. The jaeger company was gradually strengthened over the years until it was reorganized as a regiment with four companies.

Hesse-Hanau, another of the six German states which sent organized units into English service, furnished a jaeger regiment consisting of a staff of 12 persons and four companies of 100 men each in 1777 and later augmented this force with an additional company.[3]

Often employed as escorts for senior British and Hessian officers, the jaegers were generally found in the advance or rear guard forces and on special assignments, and were a vital element in most engagements; in effect, they were the green-berets of their day.

The present volume contains diary elements written by two Ansbach-Bayreuth jaeger officers. The diary of Lieutenant/Captain Heinrich Carl Philipp von Feilitzsch covers a period from March 1777, when the Ansbach-Bayreuth forces departed from their home area, until Feilitzsch's return home in 1780, having been recalled by the ruler. The original manuscript is in the archives of the University of Bayreuth, Germany. This translation was made from a copy of that manuscript provided by the War Archives of the Bavarian State Archives in Munich, Germany.

Lieutenant Christian Friedrich Bartholomai was the author of numerous letters and documents which are now in the New York Public Library He sailed to America as a second lieutenant in the 1779 recruit shipment. (Men were sent to America every year to replace those who had been killed, died, or deserted.) The present volume contains an extract from his diary covering a period from December 1779 to June 1780, during which time Bartholomai participated in General Sir Henry Clinton's successful expedition against, and capture of, Charleston, South Carolina.

Editorial Procedures

In making these translations, long, involved sentences and paragraphs have been broken into shorter elements to make reading and understanding easier. The dates for diary entries have been changed to provide consistency, and a letter e has been used following the vowels, a, o, u to indicate when those letters have been written with an umlaut in the German text. The spelling of both individual and place names has been changed when the author obviously misspelled them, or to a more current spelling, when known. Finally, parentheses within the translation are as used by the authors and brackets have been used for translator notations.

No bibliography has been provided as such information is available in any library. However, several especially important sources of material covering the jaegers, the siege of Charleston, and the Hessians in general, deserve to be mentioned. They are:

Johann Ewald. Diary of the American War, A Hessian Journal (New Haven, 1979, translated and edited by Joseph P. Tustin.

Bernhard A. Uhlendorf (translator and editor). *The Siege of Charleston, With an Account of the Province of South Carolina: Diaries and Letters of Hessian Officers, from the Jungkenn Papers in the William L. Clements Library* (Ann Arbor, 1938), and

Inge Auerbach and Otto Froehlich (editors). *Hessische Truppen im Amerikanischen Unabhaengigkeitskrieg (Marburg, 1974-76)*, 5 vols. Two later volumes have been printed pertaining to the Hesse-Hanau troops.

Acknowledgments

Thanks go first to the personnel of the Bavarian State Archives and the New York Public Library for making the manuscripts available to me. Also, I wish to thank my friends in America and overseas who have encouraged me to translate the Hessian documents. Among those friends are the staff of Heritage Books, Inc., of Bowie, Maryland, who have made it possible for my translations to reach the widest possible number of persons interested in the history and development of our nation. Finally, as always, my wife Marie lent her time and knowledge so that the final product is much better than I alone could have produced.

Bruce E. Burgoyne
Dover, Delaware

Introduction

Six German states signed mutual defense treaties with England by which organized military units were placed in English service to suppress the rebellion in the American colonies. Initially Ansbach Bayreuth provided two infantry regiments and a jaeger company. The jaeger company was gradually augmented over the years, eventually resulting in the formation of a jaeger regiment.

The Authors

Heinrich Carl Philipp von Feilitzsch, born 23 April 1751, accompanied the first Ansbach-Bayreuth jaeger company to America as a lieutenant, and was promoted to captain prior to his return to Europe in early 1780. In 1797 he was appointed to a position as a senior forestry official and died 27 February 1827. He had married Margarethe Dorothea Schuler, probably after his return to Germany, and they had one son.[4]

Christian Friedrich Bartholomai sailed to America as a jaeger second lieutenant with the 1779 recruit shipment and returned to Germany in late 1782.[5]

Contents of the Diaries

The version of the Feilitzsch diary used for this translation contains a "List of Officers who Marched to America". This list includes the names, not only of all the officers who served in the Jaeger Regiment, but also the names of officers who served with the two infantry regiments. The list was obviously prepared after Feilitzsch had returned to Europe, as it includes the rank and names of persons who were promoted to officer rank in America. Also, as it lists the names of individuals in the Jaeger Regiment, which was not organized until the closing days of the war, and mentions a reorganization of the regiment in December 1783, the list may not have been made by Feilitzsch. However, because it is a part of the manuscript which was used in translating the following volume, it is included as the first part of the Feilitzsch diary.

The Feilitzsch diary presents an account of the war which covers Howe's 1777 invasion of New Jersey, the Philadelphia Campaign, the Battle of Red Bank, and the return to New York in 1778, including the Battle of Monmouth, and the 1779 engagements at Stony and Verplanck's Points. The diary also covers the sea voyage to America and the only full account that I have seen of a return to Europe while the war was still being fought. Throughout the diary there is a running account of the daily life with the military, including reports of activity in other areas and the rumors which circulated in his unit. And, like many soldiers, before and after the Revolution, he fell in love far from home. However, his dislike of the military life, and of travel on the ocean, made his American adventure one he wished never to repeat. It is interesting to note that Feilitzsch recorded Bartholomai's arrival at the company, but recorded only that the event meant more trouble for him.

When Feilitzsch sailed on his return to Europe, Bartholomai was aboard ship waiting to sail to South Carolina as part of Clinton's southern expedition. Therefore the account of jaeger activity continues without interruption. Bartholomai seems to have had a good understanding of the difficulties which England faced in waging a war in America. He also gives a detailed account of the English siege operations used to force the surrender of Charleston.

- - - - - - -

Although the loss of Charleston was one of the worst military defeats every suffered by American military forces, after General Clinton returned to New York with a large part of his command, it was only a question of time until the American army would once again control the south and end the war. Some of the jaegers were eventually captured when Cornwallis surrendered at Yorktown. Bartholomai was one of the members of Cornwallis' command who sailed aboard a flag of truce ship to New York in late 1781 to await his exchange from prisoner of war status at that place.

Lieutenant
Heinrich Carl Philipp von Feilitzsch

Diary
(1777 -1780)

Translated from a copy of the diary in the War Archives of the Bavarian State Archives in Munich, Germany.

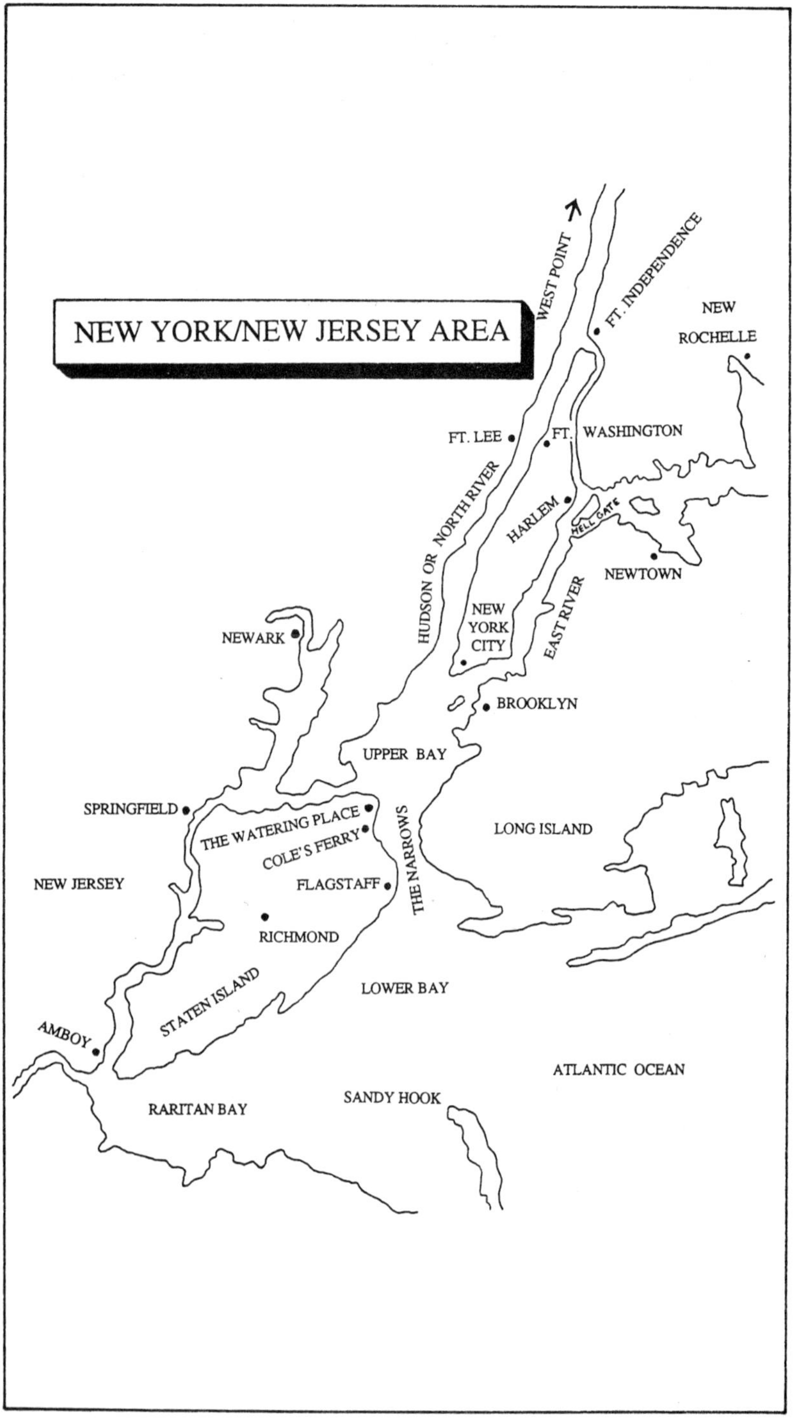

NEW YORK/NEW JERSEY AREA
WEST POINT
FT. INDEPENDENCE
NEW ROCHELLE
FT. LEE
FT. WASHINGTON
HUDSON OR NORTH RIVER
HARLEM
HELL GATE
NEWTOWN
NEW YORK CITY
EAST RIVER
NEWARK
BROOKLYN
UPPER BAY
SPRINGFIELD
THE WATERING PLACE
COLE'S FERRY
THE NARROWS
LONG ISLAND
NEW JERSEY
FLAGSTAFF
RICHMOND
STATEN ISLAND
LOWER BAY
AMBOY
ATLANTIC OCEAN
SANDY HOOK
RARITAN BAY

List of [Ansbach-Bayreuth] Officers who Marched to America

I. Illustrious Jaeger Corps

Commandant, His Excellence, Franz Carl Georg von Schilling-Constadt[1]

Major Diedrich Ernst Georg Spiegel von Pickelsheim
Captain Christian Ernst von Waldenfels
Captain Christian Ernst Voit von Salzburg
Captain Joseph Christian Friedrich von Waldenfels
Lieutenant Heinrich Carl Philipp von Feilitzsch
Lieutenant Friedrich Ebenauer

II. Illustrious Infantry Regiments:

1. Of Colonel von Voit[2]

Colonel Commandant Friedrich August Valentin Voit von Salzburg

Lieutenant Colonel Christoph Ludwig Rudolph Baron von Reitzenstein

Major Friedrich Philipp von Seitz[3]
Captain Christian Philipp von Ellrod[4]
Captain Heinrich Carl Baron von Stein zum Rechtenstein
Captain Lieutenant Friedrich Wilhelm von Roeder
1st Lieutenant Ernst Tritschler-Falkenstein
1st Lieutenant August Christian Baron von Koenitz
1st Lieutenant Friedrich Wilhelm Baron von Reitzenstein
1st Lieutenant Carl Friedrich Rudolph von Schoenfeld
1st Lieutenant Moritz Wilhelm von der Heydte
1st Lieutenant Friedrich von Keller
1st Lieutenant Wilhelm Friedrich Marschhall von Biberstein
1st Lieutenant Carl Alexander von Weitereshausen
2nd Lieutenant Justus von Diemar
2nd Lieutenant Friedrich Feder
2nd Lieutenant Georg Friedrich Philipp von Guettenberg
2nd Lieutenant Johann Ernst Prechtel

Lower Staff

Auditor - Lieutenant Johann Jakob Conrad Rummel
Regimental Quartermaster - Johann Heinrich Hartmann Model
Regimental Surgeon - Friedrich Jakob Rapp
Chaplain - Johann Conrad Wagner

2. Of Colonel von Eyb, later of von Seybothen[5]

Colonel Commandant Franz Johann Heinrich Wilhelm Christian von Seybothen
Major Ernst Friedrich Carl von Beust
Captain Friedrich Ludwig von Eyb
Captain Christian Theodor von Molitor
Captain Georg Heinrich von Quesnoy
Captain Lieutenant Friedrich Christoph Heinrich von Metsch[6]
1st Lieutenant Wilhelm Friedrich von Kruse
1st Lieutenant Johann Christoph Seidel
1st Lieutenant Philipp Otto Heinrich von Beust
1st Lieutenant Carl Friedrich von Adelsheim
1st Lieutenant Ludwig Heinrich Baron von Reitzenstein
1st Lieutenant Maximilian von Streit
1st Lieutenant Albert Ernst Ludwig Trechsel von Teufstettin
2nd Lieutenant Wilhelm von Diemar
2nd Lieutenant Georg Gustav Lebrecht von Tunderfeld
2nd Lieutenant Heinrich Altenstein
2nd Lieutenant Heinrich Weinhardt
2nd Lieutenant Adolph Daniel von Strahlendorf
2nd Lieutenant Georg Friedrich Sigismund Nagler
2nd Lieutenant [Andreas Gottlieb] von Cyriatzy[7]
2nd Lieutenant [Hermann] Lindemeyer

Lower Staff

Auditor - Lieutenant Johann Friedrich Herrnbauer
Regimental Quartermaster - Johann Georg Daig
Regimental Surgeon - Andreas Friedrich Pflug
Chaplain - Johann Philipp Erb

III. Illustrious Field Jaeger Regiment (entered Bayreuth on 9 December 1783 with the 3rd Ansbach contingent and at the same time four companies were reduced and it was divided into two regiments.[8]

Colonel Commandant S.T. Christoph Ludwig Rudolph Baron von Reitzenstein
Captain Christoph Friedrich Joseph von Waldenfels
Captain Carl Christian Ernst Tritscher von Falkenstein
Captain August Christian Friedrich von Koenitz
Captain Ernst Wilhelm Friedrich Adolf von Wurmb
Captain Lieutenant Friedrich Wilhelm Baron von Reitzenstein
Captain Lieutenant Carl Friedrich Rudolph von Schoenfeld
1st Lieutenant Moritz Wilhelm von der Heydte
1st Lieutenant Friedrich Ernst Baron von Reitzenstein
1st Lieutenant Justus von Diemar
2nd Lieutenant Christian Friedrich Bartholomai
2nd Lieutenant Jakob Ernst Kling
2nd Lieutenant Justus Hermann De Ahna
2nd Lieutenant Ehrenfried Hannes Friedrich Ferdinand Busch
2nd Lieutenant Joseph Bach
2nd Lieutenant Ferdinand von Heller
2nd Lieutenant Friedrich Adolf Carl von Eyb
2nd Lieutenant Julius von Massenbach
2nd Lieutenant Franz Count von Bubna and Lititz
2nd Lieutenant Christian Philipp Otto, Adjutant
2nd Lieutenant Albert Magnus Frank
2nd Lieutenant August Wilhelm Neidhardt von Gniesenau
2nd Lieutenant Christian Caspar Morg

Lower Staff

Auditor - Lieutenant Johannes Paul Frisch
Regimental Quartermaster - Johann Leonhard Hausselt
Regimental Surgeon - Friedrich Sigismund Arnold
Chaplain - Georg Christoph Elias Erb

[A closely written comment of about sixteen lines, which apparently refers to activities of the individuals or units during the Wars of the First and Second Coalition and the Napoleonic Wars, is not legible enough to translate.]

March of a Body of Troops from Ansbach to America 1777

7 March 1777 - I marched with the Jaeger Corps and halted at evening at Ottenhofen. The Eyb Regiment halted at Marktbergel, and the Voit Regiment at Burgbernheim.

The 8th - We all went to Uffenheim.

The 9th - This body of troops entered Ochsenfurt in the afternoon and went aboard ships. We had to remain lying there at anchor overnight, however, because there was not enough room in the ships and we had to wait for more.

The 10th - This was a memorable day as the regiments went on land, early and without permission, where they were allowed to cook. They were then to embark; the Jaegers first and then the Eyb Regiment. When it was the turn for the Bayreuth Regiment, its grenadiers began a serious rebellion, which the others joined.[1] They fled and our corps was ordered to stop them. We were ordered to fire at them and this was done, killing some and wounding others. I encountered those being pursued at the Cloister Tueckelhausen, into which some deserters had fled, and remained there until I received orders during the evening to return to Uffenheim to allow the musketeers' hatred to cool off. During the night the Prince met me on his way to Ochsenfurt, and I arrived at Uffenheim at two o'clock in the morning with a detachment of twenty men. We remained there until we received orders to move.

The 15th - We marched to Zimmern.

The 16th - To Bettingen.[2]

The 17th - To Wertheim where we ate at noon and were again embarked, but because of a storm sailed no farther than Hasloch.

The 18th - The same [weather] and we did not travel much farther. During the evening the wind abated and we traveled all night.

The 19th - At eleven o'clock we arrived at Hanau. We had to disembark and the Hereditary Prince[3] reviewed my company. At five o'clock we continued on to Offenbach where it was necessary, because of a contrary wind, to anchor. At eleven o'clock in the night a thunderstorm arose.

The 20th - We remained lying there.

The 21st - The wind died down. We set sail and arrived at Frankfurt at two-thirty. From there we continued on until we were about a mile from Mainz,[4] where, because of the night, we anchored.

The 22nd - After twelve o'clock we sailed from there, near Kostheim, and in a quarter of an hour arrived at Stein, and at one o'clock at Mainz. After another hour there, we sailed, passing Bieberich and landed for the night about a mile above Bingen.

The 23rd - We sailed at six o'clock, stopped at Bingen, and then from there sailed to Coblenz, where we halted for the night.

The 24th - With very good weather, we passed Bonn and arrived at Cologne at five o'clock, where we halted for the night.

The 25th - We sailed from there with a fairly favorable wind and passed Dusseldorf, Pfalz, and on to about a half mile before Wesel, where we spent the night.

The 26th - At five o'clock I was sent to the commandant at Wesel and we then sailed to Emmerich, where, because of the customs, we had to halt for an hour. We then continued on to Nijmegen, arriving during the evening.

The 27th - At eight o'clock in the evening we arrived at Dordrecht and at ten o'clock received orders to join the regiments which lay at anchor about five miles away.[5]

The 28th - During the afternoon we were transferred to the English ships. Ours was called *Juno*.[6] Then the oath [to the King of England] was taken.[7] We remained lying at anchor.

The 29th - We raised the anchor early in the morning and sailed to Hellevoetsluis, where we remained throughout the next day.

The 31st - We had a small storm which was accompanied by a good wind.

The 1st of April - We passed Dover.

The 2nd - We arrived at Portsmouth.

The 3rd - We remained lying there.

The 4th and 5th - Provisions were loaded aboard ship.

The 7th - We began our miserable voyage early in the morning. We sailed with a contrary wind.

The 8th - The wind was better but very strong and continued good.

The 11th - Toward evening the wind increased considerably and during the night we had a terrible storm.

The 12th - The weather was better but I was sick for several days.

The 13th and 14th - We had very good wind and weather.

The 17th - Was calm.

The 18th - Strong winds.

The 19th - Storm.

The 20th - Strong winds.

The 21st - Storm.

The 22nd - Strong winds. During this entire period the winds were contrary. All of us were still sick. Throughout our voyage I always wished I were the poorest day laborer. God save me from the sea! It is simply impossible to describe the change from being on land to being on the sea.

The 1st of May - We had no favorable wind.

The 2nd - The wind was still from the northwest, completely contrary. Toward four o'clock in the afternoon the King's ship raised a flag which indicated land, namely the Azores, and specifically, Saint Michael. On land everything seemed pleasant. Everyone went on deck just to see it, and God, how great the pleasure will be when we can see America. During the evening the wind grew strong and we again had a storm during the night.

The 3rd - Early in the morning the wind was from the northwest and again I expected not to eat because there had already been times when there was a strong wind, when we could not cook. However, toward noon the wind slackened.

The 8th and 9th - We had good wind.

The 10th - Then it came from the west.

The 11th - Again good wind from the northeast and we sailed about seven and one-half miles per hour.

The 13th - The wind was very good, from the northeast, and I have noticed at sea, when the wind comes from the morning [the east], that it generally is dull or rainy, rather than as it is in Germany, where such a wind means good weather. At five o'clock in the afternoon we saw a whale, something noteworthy.

The 15th - The wind was still favorable, from the southeast, but very weak.

The 18th - The wind was very good. During the afternoon Lieutenant [Julius von] Diemar's servant, [Peter], fell overboard from the ship *Myrtle*.[8] Because it was not very far from us, we were able to see how they pulled him out of the water, but it was to no avail. They threw him back overboard at once.

The 20th - The wind was very good, coming from the southeast by south.

The 21st - During the afternoon the favorable wind changed and came from the west. We had a hard rain. We were near the 55th degree of north longitude. The wind swung to the south during the night.

The 22nd - A very strong south wind.

The 23rd - Southwest [wind].

The 24th - Northwest [wind].

The 25th - An absolutely contrary west wind.

The 27th - Heavy rain with a south wind. We had a frightful storm during the night which tore the mainsail on the middle mast. Shortly thereafter a part of the rudder broke, causing great danger because that meant that this storm was stronger than the one on 11 April.

The 28th - A northeast wind and a dreadful storm so that again we could not cook.

The 29th - A north-northwest wind and the storm continued

The 30th - The wind was contrary, from the direction we wished to sail, the northwest.

The 31st - Southwest wind but beautiful weather. During the afternoon an American ship approached, but after the warship signaled for it to come to us, it sailed off to the south and, because it was getting dark, it could not be overtaken.

The 1st of June - Beautiful weather and a wind from the south-southwest.

The 2nd - It rained a little during the morning. The lead was cast for the first time and bottom was found at 25 fathoms.

The 3rd - Toward two o'clock in the afternoon we passed The Narrows, not far from Sandy Hook. When we saw the land early in the morning we were so pleased that no one thought about going below in the ship, as no one can fully understand who has not himself been to sea. At four o'clock we anchored near New York but unfortunately we were cheated of our hope and were not landed.

The 5th - We sailed away in the afternoon and anchored at about six o'clock at Staten Island. We were immediately disembarked. The captain and both [other] officers had remained in New York. Therefore I was greatly embarrassed, and because of the night could not get 51 of the men on land. We spent this night under the open sky for the first time.

The 6th - The remaining men debarked this morning. I had the camp set up. The captain, the officers, and the remaining men came from New York.

The 8th - At twelve o'clock at night an alarm arose near the [Ansbach-Bayreuth] Infantry. We moved out to a steady firing. However, we saw nothing although one jaeger was missing.

The 9th - He was found wounded.

The 11th - We broke camp. I was in the rear guard. We marched to the water opposite Amboy. The company and the regiments were carried across. However, because of the approaching night, I had to remain there.

The 12th - I was carried across with a detachment. At seven o'clock in the evening I marched to Brunswick, under the cover of an infantry detachment.

The 13th - I arrived at daybreak, but as the company was already several miles ahead at a landing , I moved out at once and joined it at eight o'clock.

This entire province is called New Jersey.[9] Because I had not slept for five nights, I was very tired and slept until nine o'clock at night, when the entire army moved out. We marched throughout the night.

The 14th - At noon we arrived at Hillsborough.[10] A detachment of English engaged the enemy. During the evening Captain [Johann] Ewald of the Hessian Jaegers and I were sent to Millstone, an outpost commanded by Colonel [Carl Emil Ulrich von] Donop.[11]

The 18th - Our picket was attacked by the enemy. However, as usual, they were driven back with light casualties on our side.

The 19th - The entire army marched back to Brunswick. We halted not far from the landing.

The 22nd - We moved out. I was in a flanking patrol which the enemy attacked with a heavy fire, but which failed to wound any of our men. The enemy, on the other hand, had to pull back with a number of dead and wounded, and we arrived fortunately not far from Amboy.

The 25th - I went on picket duty. Toward evening about 2,000 enemy infantry and cavalry attacked. The entire [Jaeger] Corps at once came to my support. It was a sharp engagement. We lost no one, however, and the enemy again had to retreat with losses.

The 26th - The entire army moved forward in two columns. The enemy had occupied every height. The two columns charged against them. Our losses were not large, while the enemy lost four cannons and many dead and wounded. This occurred near West Litt.

The 28th - We arrived at our former place at Amboy. (Here I must add that America is a beautiful and fruitful land, although war is ruining everything. No inhabitant is home; all the houses have been burned. In effect it now appears as if sustaining life will require an unimaginable effort. God must do His best here. I can not adequately describe how my only wishes are to be in Germany.)

The 1st of July - We moved out and were carried back to Staten Island from New Jersey, and remained overnight about a mile from that place.

The 2nd - We marched to Cole's Ferry. There we rested, safe from all enemies, and for the first time could sleep. However, we did not have much to eat except what we bought at a dear price. For diversion we hunted, shot woodcock, partridge, and rabbits, of which there are a great many. However, they are much smaller than in Europe, especially the partridge and rabbits. The former are about like the large quail, and the rabbits somewhat larger than the squirrels. I also noticed many types of trees, but because I did not know English, the names are still unknown to me.

The 9th - Unfortunately we were embarked again without knowing where we were bound.

The 19th - We still lay at anchor not far from Cole's Ferry. The whole fleet received orders to be prepared to set sail. General [William] Howe ordered, on fear of death, that no one plunder anything which he might be tempted to take in the province [of Pennsylvania], because he, [Howe], was convinced that the inhabitants, upon our landing, would revert to their allegiance. Our ship was called *Martha*.

The 20th - We set sail about ten o'clock in the morning. We had a contrary wind and could do nothing but tack. At nine o'clock in the evening we anchored behind Sandy Hook, in Raritan Bay, with New Jersey in view.

The 23rd - We set sail at nine o'clock with a west wind. Our course was toward the east and this day on the ship *Martha*, Captain [Carl August von] Wrede was in command and under his command were Lieutenant [Friedrich A.J.] von Wangenheim, Lieutenant Schaeffer, and I.

The 25th - We sailed south to Pennsylvania. We thought we were going to Philadelphia.

The 26th - The wind was contrary and very strong from early in the morning until the next morning. Once again I realized what an unfortunate life it is at sea.

The 28th - Heavy fog and at ten o'clock thunder storms and rain, and then a strong wind from the east. At six o'clock in the evening the thunder resumed and at seven o'clock we had a frightful weather. Here I will add something. Storms here in America are much stronger and last longer than in Europe. A storm is therefore much more dangerous because our fleet consists of about 300 ships, more or less, and when there is such weather it is usually accompanied by strong winds, making it difficult for the ships to sail in company. Up to this point we had remained fortunate. God will continue to help.

The 29th - The wind was from the northwest, very strong and good. However, I did not feel well and I considered my fate again and sincerely wished I were back in Germany. Who knows where we are bound? This day we passed Delaware. We changed our course toward Pennsylvania and believed we were going to Virginia. How much heat will we have to tolerate there? The experience will certainly calm our curiosity. At eight o'clock in the evening, Admiral [Lord Richard] Howe turned, unexpectedly, and we sailed directly for the Delaware.

The 30th - At six o'clock the land was clearly visible and at seven o'clock we were in Delaware Bay. The wind was contrary and we had to tack. We had beautiful weather. The sea was very restless, however, and during the evening we sailed [back] into the ocean.

The 31st - We had beautiful and good weather. We sailed first here and then there. We had the most favorable wind for entering the

Delaware, but we remained on the ocean. A strong wind arose at seven o'clock in the evening and we sailed due south.

The 1st of August - There was a west wind and we were already far out to sea by morning. We still sailed southward toward Virginia. No one any longer knew where we were bound. Everyone said something different and everyone had to leave the decision to General Howe. We still had the strong south wind and were on a westerly course. Throughout this period the weather was beautiful and we believed we were heading for Baltimore. Captain [Christoph Gustav] von Cramon and his company were on the ship *Two Brothers*. At seven o'clock in the evening we had a thunderstorm which lasted two hours. It rained very hard and the night was exceptionally dark, with a weak wind.

The 4th - Still the same wind, but very weak. It was extremely hot. About six o'clock in the evening the wind increased and at twelve o'clock we had a heavy thunderstorm.

The 5th - A west wind by which we sailed to the south on this day. Although we are hardly thirty English miles from the Delaware, I still believe that we are going to Philadelphia and that this maneuvering is only a subterfuge in order to get the rebels away from the Delaware and, upon news of that, we will at once enter. During the evening at eight o'clock there was frightful lightning, such as is never seen in Germany. It rained hard all during the night.

The 6th - Dull weather and almost no wind. I will very briefly record my thoughts on this day concerning life at sea. Anyone who has a desire to experience misery and misfortune should go aboard ship. Everyone can believe me that when I am again in Europe, should the opportunity arise for another such trip, I would certainly not go. 1) There is no bread except zwieback which is spoiled or full of worms. 2) Stinking water with all possible impurities mixed in, because on this trip, from the beginning until now, we have not had one good drop. 3) The meat is miserable and frightfully salted so that it can hardly be eaten, and then one nearly dies of thirst. 4) The entire ship is full of lice, and when it storms no one can think of anything else. Anyone who has never gone to sea can not understand how miserable that can be. It is nearly impossible to take a step without risk of breaking your neck or a leg. Everything has to be securely fastened and still everything breaks and busts to pieces. If there is no wind the water is generally restless, which causes the ship to sway back and forth in one place in a dreadful manner. There is seldom a day when a person is satisfied, but how can I describe all of it as it is? God will surely help to return me to my fatherland. During the evening, at about six o'clock, there was a thunderstorm in the distance, accompanied by rain.

The 7th - Beautiful weather but excessively warm. We saw land which we considered to be Maryland, but we sailed on into the sea. During the evening there was frequent lightning but the weather remained pleasant.

The 8th - Beautiful weather, very warm, good wind, and we sailed rapidly. The mate was very sick with a high putrid fever, very contagious, and lying not far from my bed. One can imagine how pleasant all of that is in the year 1777. Let me note here also, that the days are much shorter than in Europe, because now it is daylight about three o'clock and about, or just after seven o'clock it is again night. On this day we saw a great many different fish.

The 9th - Beautiful weather, warm, a good wind with which we sailed rapidly. We were below the 38th degree of latitude and hoped soon to reach land, which I wished from the bottom of my heart. Today we reached Cape Henry and we expect to enter tomorrow.

The 10th - Beautiful weather but with contrary wind. At about one-thirty in the afternoon the mate died. I must admit that I was glad, because he could not have recovered and was no longer able to resist death. At five o'clock in the afternoon he was buried at sea. This took place in the following manner -- He was laid on a board to which twelve cannonballs had been tied. The second mate gave a short speech in English and finally asked some sailors if this death occurred naturally and not in a violent manner. They answered this with a yes and then the body was thrown overboard.

The 11th - Beautiful weather with contrary wind and we had to tack. About six o'clock in the evening today became memorable to me. A year earlier this accident would have affected my mind. However, since my first sea voyage on the ocean, when everything seemed miserable and unusual, I have accepted that as long as I am in America, everything will be different and consider this as something to be expected. Therefore, for this reason, this incident did not affect me as much as otherwise.

A large East Indiaman ship of about 800 tons, which had 1,000 English troops on board, and was three times larger than our ship, which had only 200 men on board, sailed directly at us with a strong wind and full sails. Everyone called for the ship's captain and mate, even while it was some distance from us. It did not turn and it appeared it would run us down. That ship, fortunately, only wiped out the after part of our ship. Two large sails with all their rigging and a small boat were smashed and broken into many pieces. The so-called bowsprit or nose of the other ship penetrated about two yards into our cabin. The force can be imagined of a piece of wood going through a solid wall. On the other ship our anchor tore out a large piece of the cabin. Other than that, we know of nothing. All the jaegers and grenadiers reacted to the call and the terrible, frightful cracking on the deck. Everyone threw up his hands and shouted for help. Everyone can imagine how such an event seemed without my describing it further. The surgeon's mate from the Hessian Jaegers jumped from our ship onto the other ship. God, however, helped us out of this great danger. The ship's captain assured us that if it had hit at the middle of the ship, instead of the after part, we would all have been lost. I was prepared for anything, even this, but God helped us once again.

The 12th - Beautiful weather but a contrary southwest wind. At five o'clock we saw land at a great distance. It was Cape Charles, but because of the contrary wind we had to sail out into the sea. At twelve o'clock [at night] we turned back toward land.

The 14th - At daybreak we saw land but as the wind was still contrary, we sailed out to sea. However, at eleven o'clock we again turned toward land. Then we were caught in a calm. It was excessively warm today. About six o'clock in the evening we saw land. It was the tip of Cape Charles. At this time we fired a heavy cannonade. We anchored between eleven and twelve o'clock at night.

The 15th - At six o'clock in the morning we raised anchor and at ten-thirty, with great pleasure and quite clearly, we finally saw Cape Henry. However, at this time the fleet also anchored because the ebb tide was running against us. At one-thirty we again set sail and despite a heavy cannonade entered Chesapeake Bay. We also saw smoke and some ships. We assumed it to be frigates from our fleet engaged with the enemy but could not tell if the enemy were on water or on land. We anchored at eight o'clock. There was very strong lightning.

The 16th - We sailed at six o'clock and anchored at ten. At one-thirty we sailed and by three o'clock we were completely within Chesapeake Bay. This afternoon we had a sharp east wind with which we sailed six or seven miles per hour. We saw Virginia to the right and left, and at six o'clock we had to anchor. During the night there was a thunderstorm such as has never been seen in Europe.

The 17th - At a quarter to seven we sailed, and as usual, anchored at ten o'clock. We remained lying here all day. During the evening, almost every day, we had a thunderstorm and could not continue sailing.

The 18th - At five-thirty we again set sail. The wind was quite good. We had an indescribable heat. A contrary wind arose in the afternoon and we tacked until two o'clock. We then anchored and lay there.

The 19th - We sailed at eight o'clock and had the usual day. This was a rainy day with thunder. I also heard today that a few days ago, lightning struck an English ship, killing four dragoons and six horses.

The 21st - Today was like all the others and I know of nothing noteworthy to write. Yesterday we passed Annapolis, a beautiful place. We saw two batteries on which the English flag was flying. Today we received the order to continue onward. As of today we had 21 English miles to reach Baltimore and therefore hoped soon to disembark.

The 22nd - On this day we sailed quite close to the land on our right side. We saw many people. Today we had Baltimore behind us and sailed in another direction. We still did not know where we were bound. We anchored at six o'clock in the evening.

The 23rd - We lay still. Some ships set sail but we did not know where. At five o'clock a frigate fired a cannon shot toward land and chased the people, who had ridden to the water's edge, away. At once we saw cannon fire, on land in the distance, against our ships, which then replied. The point of land where we lie is called Turkey Point, Kent Island. Today a jaeger from the Major's Company died and was immediately thrown in the water.[12]

The 24th - We still lay at anchor here. During the afternoon we received an order to disembark tomorrow morning at three o'clock, that is, the English Grenadiers and Light Infantry, and the Hessian Jaegers and us. These are the First Brigade and are to be the first ashore.

The 25th - We entered the flatboats at two o'clock in the morning. The First Brigade formed and sailed eight miles into the Elk River. The entire fleet sailed behind us and at ten o'clock we arrived at Elk Point, where we landed. We occupied the heights at once, without seeing a single rebel. Later we marched three miles. The heat was terrible. A Hessian jaeger dropped dead and I was sick myself.

The 26th - We remained in place and during the night had a heavy rain.

The 27th - Still here and still raining. This afternoon I came off picket duty and the weather improved.

The 28th - At three o'clock we march. I had the advance guard and soon ran into the rebels. After a few shots, they retreated. We took a few prisoners. Not far from Elkton an officer of our corps took fourteen ships, on which there was sugar, coffee, tobacco, and other provisions, and also a great amount of silver products from Philadelphia. The value was estimated at one million guilders.[13] This day we marched about eight miles.

The 29th - At daybreak our outposts were attacked and about every half-hour thereafter.

The 30th - At one o'clock in the afternoon a strong enemy patrol skirmished with the pickets.

The 31st - I went on picket duty. Here I must say that this region of Maryland does not appeal to me. Compared with other provinces where we have been, this region is not well-developed. A bare woods, here and there a small place with a house and field, but where not a soul is to be seen. How desolate it is I will let another describe. It was a quiet day.

September

The 1st of September - It was exceptionally hot. During the night there was a false alarm when a jaeger deserted his post and ran back into camp, claiming that the rebels were coming and were only three hundred yards from us. This was all untrue.

The 2nd - We lay here quietly.

The 3rd - We marched out of our camp at four o'clock in the morning. At a distance of about two and one-half miles we entered Pennsylvania and shortly thereafter encountered an enemy corps of 3,000 men in the region of Wellstreg, or the Fort Euren Kill, or Katschers Mill.[14] The enemy stood firm. The fire was extremely heavy and lasted about two hours. Only our corps was engaged and a few English. The enemy attacked three times. We lost one dead and ten wounded, while the rebels suffered nearly fifty dead and, according to the deserters, very many wounded. We made few prisoners. Our jaegers conducted themselves well and, after the enemy was driven back, we entered camp during the afternoon not far from that place. The affair began at eight o'clock and lasted until ten. The company had two wounded, a corporal and a jaeger.

The 4th - I went on picket duty. Everything remained quiet.

The 5th - We remained in place.

The 6th - Still here. We saw nothing but one enemy patrol.

The 7th - We still remained here.

The 8th - We moved out at five o'clock in the morning. We marched about seven miles along a route not suspected by the enemy, although he had obstructed the obvious route with chopped-down trees and entrenchments. During the entire day the flanking patrols only fired about a dozen shots.

The 9th - I went on picket duty. At five o'clock in the evening we moved out and marched throughout the entire night.

The 10th - At nine o'clock in the morning we arrived at King's Crossing. At three o'clock in the afternoon we again moved out and again entered camp not far from that place.

I must note here in Pennsylvania, that the inhabitants are encountered everywhere. The province is more loyal to the King than all the others. Therefore nothing is taken from the inhabitants. It is not more heavily populated than the others. Since the storms have let up, it has rained less and almost not at all.

The 11th - We marched at four o'clock in the morning. At eleven o'clock we halted in a woods in order to first reconnoiter the enemy. An hour later we resumed our march until two o'clock, when we again halted because no one knew where or how the enemy was located. During this time we heard a heavy cannonade from near where we had been in the morning. This was General [Wilhelm] von Knyphausen, who had gone a different way with the first column and attacked the enemy's left wing. That was only a feint, however, to draw the enemy's attention to himself until both columns could attack at the same time. At three-thirty our advance guard encountered the enemy. At once the army marched into battalion order. Our corps entered the line on the end of the left wing. At exactly four o'clock the battle began. The small arms fire was terrible, the counter-fire from the enemy, especially against us, was the most concentrated. All the battalions made the attack. The enemy had made a good disposition with one height after the other to his rear. He stood fast and was certainly four times as strong as we were. However, all the English and Hessians conducted themselves as they are well-known to do. They attacked with great strength and with the bayonet. The enemy was defeated and had to retreat. [The battle] lasted until seven o'clock and during their flight, Knyphausen sharply cannonaded them. Our company suffered four wounded and five dead, including one officer who will surely die later.[15] The loss for the entire army amounts to about 500 men. The enemy loss can not be determined because, in so far as possible, they took their wounded with them. Still their losses are much greater than ours according to the statements of the many deserters. They also lost fourteen cannons, one howitzer, and one field culverin. The battalions took post on Brandywine Hill not far from Brandywine Town, or Delanot. At eight o'clock in the evening we entered camp not far from that place. Once again God has helped us.[16]

The 12th - We remained in place. Many prisoners and deserters were brought in on this day.

The 13th - Everything was quiet until our corps marched off at three o'clock in the afternoon. However, we went no more that a couple of miles to where we had usually had our outposts. We heard that our fleet had advanced to Wilmington on the Delaware.

The 14th - Everything remained peaceful and calm. We heard cannon fire in the distance.

The 15th - We remained in our present camp.

The 16th - At five o'clock in the morning we marched. At twelve o'clock there was a heavy rain and at two o'clock we encountered the enemy. There was heavy firing on all sides. We drove them back, and they lost four dead, two wounded, and twenty men taken captive. We moved into camp at that place. It rained extremely hard during the night.

The 17th - We had a day of rest. I went on picket duty. At five o'clock the order came to march. We were ready to march when the order came to remain where we were.

The 18th - At three o'clock we moved out. We again made contact with an enemy patrol, which retreated with losses. After we had marched about ten miles, we made camp.

The 19th - We remained in place, and the weather was beautiful again.

The 20th - We were to march but were informed of a large enemy supply depot and so remained in place. At one o'clock during the night, the English attacked a large enemy corps which was to have attacked our flank during the march. Five hundred men were killed and wounded on the spot and 200 were captured. The remainder escaped to the enemy camp without weapons.[17]

The 21st - We marched after the enemy at three o'clock in the morning, but as we did not know exactly where they were, we halted. [General] Howe sent a scouting party out under a pretext. We entered camp during the evening.

The 22nd - I went on picket duty. Later we went on patrol with the entire army but saw nothing of the enemy. However, shortly thereafter they often approached and were observed. During the afternoon a strong detachment of jaegers and grenadiers crossed the water toward the enemy. First there was a heavy cannonade and throughout the night the outposts exchanged fire. We also began building bridges in order to make the enemy believe we would attack at this place. At ten o'clock at night, at my picket but not under my responsibility, a great alarm occurred in the corps, and nearly in the whole army, because a woman attempted to flee [to the enemy]. At twelve o'clock we marched back to our former camp. The night was exceptionally cold.

The 23rd - We had to cross the Schuylkill near Watts Ford. The troops had to wade across with the water up to their body. About two o'clock we entered camp on the road to Philadelphia. Attractive and splendid houses were to be seen here, but few inhabitants.

The 24th - We had a day of rest. About eleven o'clock an enemy patrol approached and delivered a sharp fire against our foragers, but without damage. On this side of the river we could see their pickets on a hill. Today I heard also that our English Light Dragoons captured an iron cannon and a flag which a small detachment of the enemy had abandoned when the Dragoons entered the rebels' camp.

The 25th - At eight o'clock in the morning we marched from our camp to Murring Town. We passed this day very peacefully and without seeing a single rebel. Here we saw as beautiful a region as is to be seen in all America. The wilderness ends and three or four houses stand near one another. Except for the Quakers, all have fled. Here mostly Germans lived. The region is hilly and stony. It rained heavily all afternoon and into the night. At five o'clock we entered camp near the Falls of the Schuylkill. From here it was five English miles to Philadelphia.

The 26th - We had a day of rest. Today two English and two Hessian grenadier battalions were placed in a brigade under the command of General Lord [Charles] Cornwallis, so they could march to Philadelphia and take possession of the city.

The 27th - From nine to eleven o'clock we heard heavy cannon fire on the Delaware, where we heard our side had raised a battery which two enemy ships had engaged. I made a patrol with fifty jaegers under the command of General [Charles] Gray. However, we did not see any rebels.

The 28th - We still lay quietly [in camp].

The 29th - I went on picket duty. The next morning at three o'clock, while it was still very dark, a young person of about twenty years of age approached the outer sentry very hastily. The sentry challenged him three times, but he gave no answer, and continued to come nearer. The sentry fired and shot him dead on the spot.

The 30th - At nine o'clock in the morning I had this unfortunate individual buried.

The 1st of October - Everything remained quiet. It appeared as if we would remain here for a long time. I wish to Heaven the campaign were finished and that we would have the very much wished-for peace, and that in the coming spring we will be able to return to our fatherland in Europe.

The 2nd - We received the order to be prepared to move out at a moment's notice.

The 3rd - We heard that the enemy was very near us.

The 4th - At daybreak we heard our pickets fire. We moved out at once and then heard a heavy cannonade on the army's right wing toward Germantown. The enemy drove our pickets back; we moved forward. The enemy fire against us from both cannons and small arms was heavy. We answered ineffectually with our rifles because we were too far from them. However, after three hours, we heard that our good English allies had repulsed the enemy. We then advanced causing the enemy to take flight. Our corps lost eleven wounded, but the company did not lose a single man. Thank God! However, the army lost 250 men, dead and wounded. The enemy had about 13,000 men, but our army was very weak. No one will believe when I say what our strength was, because of the many necessary posts we had to occupy. The enemy losses in dead, wounded, and captured amounted to about 2,000 men. Fifty-one officers were captured. I went on picket duty.[18]

The 5th - It was reported that the enemy was 24 English miles from here and had a desire to attack us once again with his whole army. Surely God will protect us.

The 6th - We remained quiet.

The 7th and 8th - The same.

The 9th - At two o'clock in the morning the picket alerted us and at three o'clock I marched to relieve the picket. This day we learned that the enemy had marched to Parringtown and still desired attacking us again. At twelve o'clock at night I had another fatality when a private in the relief force approached a guard and was accidently shot. This seriously bothered me because he was a very good man.

The 10th - We remained here peacefully until evening, when we received the order to be under arms at three o'clock the following morning.

The 11th - We moved out again at three o'clock in the morning and heard from a returning patrol that very many rebels had been seen in a woods about three English miles ahead of us. One corporal and three men of the patrol had been captured. We remained in place until about nine o'clock and then broke ranks. However, once or twice during the night we had to fall out with our weapons.

The 12th - At eleven-thirty an enemy patrol was seen on the other side of the Schuylkill. They fired a few shots at our outposts near the river. Every day we hear the cannons on the enemy ships firing against our troops who are in the batteries on the Delaware River. This firing continues day and night and we hope that God will help us there and finally get us out of America.

The 13th - Everything remained quiet. I heard that Lieutenant von Forstner, who lay wounded at Wilmington, had died.

The 14th - I went on picket duty and made a patrol under Captain von Wrede. Our mounted jaegers saw only five of the enemy, who did not wait for us, however. I certainly have not had such a peaceful picket for a long time.

The 15th - I was relieved at eight o'clock and was still on my way [back to camp] when I heard an enemy patrol firing across the Schuylkill at our pickets.

The 16th - We saw and heard nothing but a strong cannonade on the Delaware, which did not last very long.

The 17th and 18th - Everything was quiet. At twelve o'clock at night I went on picket duty.

The 19th - In the morning I received an order to become the rear guard when the corps moved out. At nine o'clock an enemy cavalry patrol approached, and after ten o'clock the entire army marched away. We moved forward three miles toward Philadelphia. After we made camp, I went on picket duty. It was excessively hot today.

The 20th - I was relieved at eight o'clock in the morning. It had been a long [tour of duty] on picket. At ten o'clock at night the order came to be ready to march at three o'clock in the morning.

The 21st - We marched early and passed through Philadelphia before daylight. Close to the city we were loaded into flatboats and at daybreak were landed on the other side, in Jersey, near Cooper's Ferry, where we saw about thirty enemy. They retreated after a few shots. We remained there until about three o'clock when we marched to

Haddonfield. Underway we received a few shots. At seven o'clock in the evening we arrived. Our commander was Colonel von Donop and our entire corps consisted of three grenadier battalions and one musket battalion. My captain [von Cramon], who had not been well for some time, remained in Philadelphia, to my very great sorrow; in part for his person and also because of the company opportunities [which he would miss by not being in the coming battle].

The 22nd - At four o'clock in the morning we marched, and at about ten o'clock arrived at our assigned place near Fort Red Bank. Immediately preparations were begun for storming the fort, and when everything was ready, at about four o'clock, it began. However, the commandant would not surrender so the attack was launched. The cannonade was severe and the small arms fire very heavy. In addition, several rebel ships joined in, which fired against us on both sides and did great damage. The attack continued a long time, until finally our good Hessian grenadiers had to retreat. (We had only field pieces with us and I do not know what else we were lacking.) This time we jaegers had no part except to cover the rear. Our losses consisted of Colonel von Donop, who remained lying wounded at the fort, another 26 officers, who were dead and wounded, and about 350 privates. The exact number was not immediately known. During the night we marched back six miles, arriving at one o'clock.[19]

The 23rd - We continued our march at three o'clock, arriving at Cooper's Ferry. I was very sick and miserable. The march was made very quickly and we had nothing to eat. It was my fate to be very indisposed, and I wished to Heaven to be away from there and back home. On this day we also received the sad news that a warship, which had exchanged fire with the second fort,[20] had blown up and that a frigate that was there grounded on a sandbank and had to be set afire. We remained lying there until nine o'clock at night, when we fortunately were shipped across. While still dark, we marched through the city and at one o'clock entered our former camp.

The 24th - Everything quiet.

The 25th - I went on picket duty and was feeling a bit better.

The 26th - At eight o'clock in the morning I was relieved. It began to rain very hard. During the night we were alerted five times. This day we changed our camp. Wrede's Company and ours were moved to another height.

The 27th - Heavy rain and wind and terrible weather in which to lie in a tent under the open sky, as I had to do.

The 28th - Still the same type of weather. It rained even harder. The wind increased and did not letup all day. It is completely different than in Germany.

The 29th - Still the same weather. We believed the jaegers and all of us would die.

The 30th - At four o'clock in the morning I went on picket duty and, thank God, it quit raining, although there was still a strong wind throughout the day. There is a shortage of provisions and food which can be bought. The inhabitants bring us nothing and the rations are the worst imaginable. On their faces their malice and hatred toward us can be seen. We are not allowed to take the least thing here in the province, nor to do anything to them. This only increases their evil the more, and therefore we have to be more careful of the farmers than of the enemy soldiers.

The 31st - Beautiful weather. I was told today that Colonel von Donop had died in the enemy's hands. However, his adjutant, Captain [Johann Emanuel] Wagner, was brought to Philadelphia very dangerously wounded. The total loss before the fort was 377 men, including 23 officers, dead and wounded.

The 1st of November - Beautiful weather but very cold. The captain and nearly half the company unfortunately are sick. We still have no provisions. If the Delaware River were open everything would be different. Also, we learned from deserters that the rebels were also in very poor condition.

The 2nd - Beautiful weather, but otherwise nothing special.

The 3rd - Beautiful weather. Today we celebrated Lieutenant [Johannes] Heinrich's birthday. The captain was feeling better again and returned to the company.

The very sad news was received that General [John] Burgoyne, commanding in Canada, had been captured with 4,000 men, mostly Brunswick troops. Good night peace! Without God's help we will not be able to enjoy the sweet hope this year.

The 4th - I went on picket duty. It was a very beautiful day. Everything was quiet except some cavalry shot at some of our mounted jaegers. The cannonade on the Delaware was very heavy.

The 5th - I went on picket duty. A dull, raw day. The cannonade yesterday continued unceasingly, without apparent results.

The 6th - Rotten weather. It rained throughout the past night. I had previously had a board hut made for me instead of a tent. After having been disturbed during the night by some random shots, which I had to investigate, I wanted to peacefully rest in my warm house. However, after being awake for some hours, it rained through the roof onto my bed and then on my whole body. My bed was completely wet. (Note - This was made with hay and straw underneath and a wool blanket.) My chimney or fireplace smoked terribly. I almost wished again to sleep in a tent where I would have only been wet from below and cold from above. We are never content. It seems, however, we have reason [to be discontented] in America, and I still believe we have earned this right. However, I realized this too late and only wish that every young German who takes the time to read these scrawls - which anyone can see at the start that this journal was only written as a reminder to me so nothing will be forgotten - can apply the moral to himself. Then, in the future, he can think what an unhappy fate we must accept, without knowing what changes to expect in life. Everyone thinks, "I want my peace [and quiet]." A local farmer assured me that the present weather will continue; usually three days and sometimes three weeks. That would be all right if it were only like a European rain, but everyone dreads the present rain and wind. Today we received our baggage. Since landing from the ship I have had only three shirts, three pairs of stockings, and handkerchiefs; otherwise not even an overcoat. Would to God I were in my fatherland and no longer had to worry about it.

The 7th - The weather changed and was rather good.

The 8th - Beautiful weather until toward evening when it began to rain, and rained quite hard all night long.

The 9th - I went on picket duty at five o'clock in the morning. It was beautiful weather and for a change did not rain on our picket. God be praised! Reimbursement money was paid for one month. The expenses were great and there was a scarcity of foodstuffs. Because we did not have free passage for our ships, all the provisions which we received had to sneak past the enemy's Fort Mud Island at night. On this night a double outpost guard deserted from me.

The 10th - I was relieved at eight o'clock. The cannonade on the Delaware was very heavy and continued all day. It was from floating batteries which had been made by our side and which were attacked by the enemy ships lying nearby. About one o'clock it began to rain softly. Toward evening it was reported that the fire from the cannons of our batteries was being directed against the enemy fort.

The 11th - Wind and rain, and the cannonade continued without letup.

The 12th - Strong wind and very cold. Today a strong enemy patrol, which was aware of our situation, approached. We moved out but no shots were fired. The cannonade was like before.

The 13th - Very cold and continuous, strong wind. Every day, just like this morning, we were plagued by the enemy. However, he is not successful. It is reported that an enemy frigate and a row galley had surrendered to one of our previously captured frigates, which lay above Philadelphia to prevent ships from passing. However, this resulted from necessity. Still this is certain, a frigate and a provisions ship from our fleet fortunately passed over the *chevaux de frise* and the latter ship lies in the Schuylkill. It is said that our two [Ansbach] battalions are coming. Would to God that this is true.

The 14th - I went on picket duty. It was a pretty and peaceful day and not as cold.

The 15th - I was relieved in the morning. Today the cannonade was the strongest. It was difficult to distinguish the shots, but there was a constant rumble in the air. During the night a great fire could be seen in the distance.

The 16th - A very dull and cold day. At noon it began to snow. We no longer heard the cannonade. Therefore we waited for good news and heard that the warship *Vigilant* had passed over the *chevaux de frise*, two of which still lie in the river, and on the previous day had heavily damaged the fort so that the garrison therein had to set it afire and then abandon it. They retreated to the nearby Fort Red Bank, which, however, is surrounded by 4,000 of our men.

The 17th - A very cold and overcast day. We strongly wish to enter winter quarters, for which there seems little chance. During the afternoon Captain Wrede, Lieutenant Freuenhagen, and fifty men were ordered to be ready to march. They departed at eleven o'clock at night. We did not know where.

The 18th - Everything changed. Then I heard the various English battalions plus a Hessian grenadier battalion, under the command of General Cornwallis, marched to Chester, where 4,000 men already are waiting. The entire corps, consisting of 8,000 men, apparently will attack Red Bank.

The 19th - I went on picket duty. Beautiful weather and not at all cold. Our corps received the order to break camp. This happened during the morning. We moved to another height because the line had been weakened by the withdrawal of the mentioned detachment. It created a great amount of work for our troops, and even more to build the huts. We heard the news that the mentioned corps attacked a rebel corps that same morning at three o'clock, near Farby,[21] and killed 300, most of which could be credited to the Hessian battalion. However, we still have no positive news. Toward evening I had to move back to a better position with the picket. However, an enemy patrol harassed me during this time, just after darkness set in. This [patrol] engaged the post of our mounted jaegers but did not get very close to us.

The 30th - Still unpleasant weather, strong wind, and also very cold.

The 1st of December - Very cold. I rode into the city again and looked over part of it, because the city reportedly has very many interesting sights. I do not find this to be true. The city has eight long streets and sixteen cross streets, which are all laid out very regular. However, they are very narrow. The houses are very small, in part, others somewhat larger, but none of them are comparable with a well-built German house. The sympathy of the residents for the Congress, and their hatred toward us, is written on every face. What else can be expected? This nation consists mostly of those from our fatherland who were driven out as being too lazy to work or escaped hanging.

There are reports of our marching. What will that be like? It is winter, wherever we go we encounter the enemy, and everything is uncertain. But it is no better here. Bread is scarce and is available only once a week. Two pounds cost half a Convention dollar. But what can I do? It would be better for me to give it to Him who has saved me from such constant danger and has watched over us since our birth. I will eternally thank Him after He has extended His complete help in returning me to my fatherland. Our living style here is difficult to describe, even though I have been fortunate up to the present time.

The 2nd - A frightful wind. It also snowed a little this morning. The picket, as usual, sent out a patrol. (Note - The rebels were alert, wounded two of the mounted jaegers, and captured one.)

The 3rd - Nothing special. Toward midday the order to march was received.

The 4th - Suddenly we moved out from our camp at ten o'clock at night. The army, which I estimated at 9,000 to 10,000 men, was commanded by General Cornwallis. We marched throughout the night by way of Germantown.

The 5th - At six o'clock in the morning we arrived at Chestnut Hill. It was astonishingly cold. The English Light Infantry had the advance guard and constantly exchanged fire with the enemy outposts and pickets in the area. After daybreak and after we had put out our usual outposts, the enemy established a picket quite near us. We could see their camp place (in English) called White Marsh. At two o'clock in the afternoon a large enemy patrol approached and strongly attacked our picket, which was then supported by two companies of our corps. The firing was heavy but did not last long. The enemy had to retreat with losses of five dead and wounded. Our losses were three men wounded, including one man slightly wounded from our company. Shortly thereafter the Light Infantry was attacked. They were more successful. They counter-attacked with bayonets and forced the rebels back, with the loss of fifty men, dead, wounded, and captured, including General Arnim.

The 6th - We remained where we were but nothing happened. The enemy camp was very secure and well-entrenched. We marched at twelve o'clock at night. We marched back by our previous route, by way of Germantown. At this point, however, we turned left and arrived at twelve o'clock on

The 7th - at Edgehill. After resting for an hour under the command of General Grey, we counter-marched and, according to the statement of prisoners, encountered 2,500 rebels, who were hidden behind a height. We came within twenty yards of them. The firing was very heavy but they had to retreat head over heels. Our losses amounted to one dead and nine wounded. The company, God be praised, lost no one. The enemy left 42 dead behind and about ten prisoners. We chased them a short distance and then halted when the Light Infantry beside us engaged them, as usual, with a bayonet attack. Reportedly they suffered 300 killed with bayonets and 200 made prisoners. We moved back into a camp in Abington Township. At six o'clock in the evening I went on picket duty. This was a very restless night for us. The enemy was close and fired constantly at us from fear.

The 8th - I was relieved at eight o'clock in the morning. During the afternoon we heard that we would march back because the enemy was too strongly entrenched. When they became aware of this, they approached and fired heavily at our pickets. We drove them off, however, with our amusettes. We moved out at three o'clock. It remained quiet until shortly before night when they attacked the rear guard. The bullets came thickly toward our company. Later, however, we were undisturbed and arrived at our former camp at Philadelphia at nine o'clock. It was very cold, there had been little sleep, and therefore I was very tired and happy to be there, and satisfied with my fate.

The 9th - Nothing special; no rebels were seen.

The 10th - A beautiful day, but very cold. A small enemy patrol approached this morning. I went into the city to see a good friend. At nine o'clock in the evening we provided a strong detachment, including a captain. It marched at two o'clock and joined a larger detachment, commanded by General Cornwallis, amounting to 3,000 men. They crossed the Schuylkill River to go foraging as well as to seize livestock and horses.

The 11th - Today we heard a heavy cannonade but no small arms fire from the detachment. We had to get the entire army ready to move because it was reported that the enemy had moved in large numbers of men.

The 12th - We had to remain ready to move out at a moment's notice. Nothing could be heard but the very distant lone-falling cannon shots. It was a really nice day but very cold at night. Fate is catching up with me, and I have the very common ailment of scurvy in the legs. I have great pain and the swelling is pronounced. I had almost decided to request a discharge and, with God's help, to return to my fatherland, when I received a letter from my relatives. It rained hard toward evening. At eleven o'clock at night the detachment returned without having suffered any casualties. However, another was ordered out immediately.

The 13th - The detachment, as strong as that of yesterday, moved out at daybreak. The fair weather continued, but it was very cool. At evening the detachment returned.

The 14th - It was a very raw day.

The 15th - I went on picket duty. It was a beautiful day and everything remained quiet.

The 16th - As I left the picket in the morning it began to rain and this continued all day.

The 17th - It continued to rain.

The 18th - The weather improved. A jaeger deserted from the company today.

The 19th - Everything was quiet, but it was very cold.

The 20th - A very cold and windy day. We have hopes of entering winter quarters as it is snowing and the campaign has ended. I am especially happy because now some of the unpleasantness must end. Despite the most strict orders, many of the inhabitants' houses were burned down over their heads and others were plundered and everything taken. Even if these unfortunate persons at the same time have earned this treatment, through their previous life style or by their present conduct, I still do not wish to be considered an instrument in punishing them, nor even to be witness thereto. If there are those who take pleasure in such cruelties, they may take satisfaction to their fullest, as there are ample opportunities to do so.

The 21st - I was ordered to take the men of the company, who so desired, to church in the city. This was a pleasant duty for me because, since I left Germany, I have seen few churches and been in even fewer. There are not many in the countryside and those few are mostly in ruins, because most of the preachers have joined the rebels and led their parishioners into their evil beliefs. There are two Lutheran [churches] in Philadelphia, but one has been converted to a hospital. In America, especially in Pennsylvania, all possible religions are found which would not be tolerated in Europe. The Quakers are the most numerous and exercise their form of religious services most conscientiously. The others, however, for the most part, have no serious beliefs and therefore are less devout. I returned at eleven-thirty. It was a beautiful day. During the evening we received the unwished-for order to be prepared to march.

The 22nd - Very cold. At eight o'clock in the morning we marched out. The entire army marched, leaving only 1,000 men in Philadelphia. Of our men, however, only Captain Wrede and our company. We crossed the floating bridge over the Schuylkill and stopped close to it. The left wing of the army extended to the Delaware with the object of collecting all of the forage there.

The 23rd - I went on picket duty. It was rather cold and windy.

The 24th - Everything remained quiet.

The 25th - The same situation, but never in my life have I celebrated such a holiday.

The 26th - During the afternoon an enemy patrol approached and attacked the non-commissioned officer's picket. I was sent there with 24 men as a reinforcement, but the enemy at once retreated.

The 27th - Once again it began to rain and during the night changed to snow. It can well be imagined what the army had to tolerate without tents and without huts.

The 28th - I went on picket duty at six o'clock in the morning, but initially had to take an advance post until it was fully daylight. We had reports that the enemy planned to attack; however, they did not do so. At eight o'clock I pulled back to the picket and at ten o'clock received orders to march. We then moved forward a short distance to cover the army' s flank while it moved back across the floating bridge and into the former camp. I formed the rear guard with the picket. Suddenly the enemy came and attacked our cavalry posts, but were driven off. It snowed and rained today without stopping.

The 29th - It was so cold and the wind was so strong that it can never be this cold in Europe. We suffer, therefore, very much in our camp.

The 30th - We received orders to move into our quarters. At twelve o'clock we marched away. They are about two miles from the city in the region called The Neck. We were all quartered in four houses, so that the company of 74 men was in a house with two small rooms. Lieutenant [Friedrich] Ebenauer and I were together. Our room is very large and cold so that during the night, because it was so cold and we had no bed covers, we froze. Our host is a native-born German named Lutz.

The 31st - Still colder. During the night, on our straw, we had our previous fate. Today the rebels burned two of our transport ships because they were too close to land along the Delaware River and were frozen in. The English put two howitzers opposite and they were fully occupied just to save ours. I wish with all my heart that with the end of the year, all hostilities will cease and that in the new year I will have only memories, in Germany, although my fate has not been so hard as that of many others. If my system does not improve, however, I can only hope that my strength will hold out as well in the next campaign as in this one. How long will God test us in such a difficult situation even if we have earned His anger?

1778

The 1st of January - Just as cold as previously, but then somewhat better in the afternoon. I have never had such a day before at this place. I could not attend church services. In short, we are fated to live as heathens.

The 2nd - The day began with fog. Otherwise everything is peaceful and quiet.

The 3rd - The weather improved. The piles of snow disappeared.

The 4th to 6th - The weather was the same. It froze every night and thawed every day. There was a maid in my quarters, who was not very pretty, but she had lovers enough because it is like this - When the sailors come ashore I amuse myself by watching them. This often annoys them.

The 7th - It snowed and was a dull day. We received orders to visit the captain's host [1] because he had reportedly hidden ammunition for the Americans. However, we found nothing.

The 8th - I went on picket duty abut seven and one-half miles toward Gloucester, on the Delaware. It rained off and on today. **Note** - I regretted this night very much the next day.

The 9th - Beautiful weather. At eleven o'clock I was relieved.

The 10th and 11th - It snowed.

The 12th - It froze very hard. There is much talk of peace again, which I wish from the bottom of my heart. I do not believe it because if it is not my unhappy fate to remain here, nevertheless I dread the thought of the return voyage. However, I would tolerate all sorts of difficulties to see my relatives and my fatherland once again.

The 13th - A beautiful day, but very cold this morning. The day, however, is like one in May in Germany.

The 14th, 15th, and 16th - The same cold weather persisted. I went on picket duty and everything was quiet.

The 17th - I was relieved at eleven o'clock. It rained very hard today, as usual, because everything happens in extremes.

The 18th - Beautiful days until

The 23rd - There was changeable weather, extremely cold at night and then within half an hour the most beautiful spring weather. In general, an unhealthy weather and climate for us Germans. However, everything remained quiet and we lived here peacefully in our solitude and had everything we needed.

The 24th - Very cold weather.

The 25th - I went on picket duty. As it had been very cold and froze the previous night, so the sun was so warm this morning that the snow which had fallen melted within an hour.

The 30th - Nothing occurred. Today was the most beautiful summer day but no one could move from one house to another because the mud was so deep and nothing here is firm.

The 3rd of February - I went on picket duty. We received reports that the enemy would attack during the night in order to capture the picket. Therefore I was more alert than usual and at eleven o'clock we actually heard the rebel boats being put into the Delaware on the other side. They set sail but did not attack us, so everything remained quiet.

The 4th - At eleven o'clock the orders arrived that no one should go to sleep nor leave camp, apparently because an attack was expected.

The 5th - However, as I had anticipated, we were not disturbed. Currently the rebels are using strong measures to press men into the service of the militia and making all necessary preparations for the coming campaign. Hopes of peace are fading and we must also be prepared and not shy away from barbarity, regardless of how it might be considered by a European. It is necessary here and done without any thought because that is not considered as a vice here. For some days we have had the most beautiful summer days.

The 8th - Suddenly an extremely heavy snow.

The 9th - It rained very hard and water is standing in every field. Nevertheless, much of the snow still remains.

The 12th - It was very cold and windy. I went on picket duty and the standing water caused me much trouble.

The 13th - I was relieved as usual. Everything was quiet.

The 14th - The wind was still so strong and also as cold as before. The enemy who are only in huts in the field must feel it, as I could not sleep well because of the cold, even when in my bed during the past night, completely wrapped up in a wool blanket. Also, General [George] Washington, if reports are true, has pulled back to Lancaster with his regular troops because he has determined that the impressed soldiers are not trustworthy. However, I do not believe this because so many of the reports are slanted in our favor, all of which anticipate an early peace. We can believe no less than this if we have religion. However, the inhabitants among them have not been punished enough for their wicked conduct.

The 22nd - Throughout the watch the weather was very changeable.

The 23rd - When I went on watch it was raining very heavily. During the night it was very cold and suddenly it began to snow hard. In a short time the English have captured a great number of rebel officers, who have been betrayed by the farmers, because the officers have been living in the neighborhood. I can not determine the number, but to tell the truth, I would put the number at about sixty. Many of their privates also desert as does an officer, occasionally. From our newly raised provincial troops many also desert. It seems as if the rebels only wish to get uniforms from us because those in the area are poorly equipped.[2]

The 1st of March - I went on picket duty. I had the company of our newly raised militia. The captain and the lieutenant, whom I met for the first time, were with them. They told me that they had returned from New Jersey with the Light Infantry. During the past day it rained constantly, but it turned very cold during the night.

The 2nd - I was relieved. It was still very cold.

The 3rd - It snowed extremely heavily. Otherwise, however, everything remained peaceful and it was almost not worth the trouble of having us here to carry out our tasks.

The 8th - I went on picket duty. Everything was quiet.

The 9th - I was relieved as usual. Forty ships set sail for England this morning.

The 15th - We remained here completely undisturbed so that no one would believe that we hear and see nothing. During the previous watch a Hessian jaeger by the name of Pfromel was to be hanged, reportedly because he had deserted. However, because of his family, supposedly, he was pardoned and sentenced to run the guantlet twenty times. For several days we have had the most beautiful summer days. However, I fear that there will be much sickness due to the sudden warm spell. If the sun appeared before the extremely heavy fog, it would be warmer than in Europe in August. Once again I think of my relatives and immediately my spirits sink because I still have received no mail.

The 18th - I went on picket duty.

The 19th - As usual I was relieved.

The 26th - Today it began to rain. Previously, however, we had a period of the best warm weather. During this time I had the diversion of hunting woodcock, and fieldfares, a sort of thrush. The first compares closely with those in Germany but they are smaller. The second are just like those in Europe. The latter, however, which are called amsel here, are the same size as ours but gray on the back like the fieldfare in Germany. On the other hand, their belly is red and there are a great many of them.[3]

Note - The 16th - I changed quarters; the various reasons I will omit as being unnecessary to record here.

The 27th - I went on picket duty. During the afternoon a fleet of 120 ships with provisions came up the Delaware. I saw 37 of them anchor near the ferry at my picket. Our Colonel von Eyb as well as other officers and soldiers came with them, having remained behind in New York sick, (and our baggage). Next day the ships raised their anchors and sailed up to the city.

The 28th - As usual, I was relieved. When I got home I heard that a detachment of 200 of our jaegers had left during the previous night to open the road for people bringing in produce, because the rebels had threatened to hang anyone bringing food into the city. However, no enemy were encountered and they returned at ten o'clock. It was a very warm summer day.

The 29th - Rain and snow were mixed with one another and the wind was extremely cold and strong.

The 30th - The same weather. Maybe tomorrow it will be as warm as previously.

The 31st - My prophecy came true as today was a beautiful day.

The 1st of April - It was a summer day, as in August in Europe.

The 2nd - Very cold and rainy. During the evening we had a thunderstorm.

The 3rd - Again at night 200 jaegers were detached. I was included. We crossed the Schuylkill River at midnight. We marched in two columns. I went seven miles along the Forchester Road,[4] under the command of Captain von Cramon. However, as we encountered no enemy, we began our return.

The 4th - We returned at nine o'clock.

The 5th - I went on picket duty. At two o'clock two transport ships anchored at the ferry, having come from Rhode Island.

The 6th - I was relieved, but again at night a detachment was sent out in which I was included.

The 7th - We marched at five o'clock in the morning, Lieutenant [Franz Christian von] Bodungen, I, and fifty jaegers. We traveled by the previous road, about one mile beyond the Schuylkill, in order to cover the wagons used to bring produce back to the city. We met nine rebel riders, who retreated when our mounted jaegers fired at them.

At one o'clock we marched back to our quarters.

The 10th - We have had beautiful weather for quite a long time, but it is very cold at night.

The 14th - I went on picket duty.

The 15th - I heard that Colonel von Eyb and Lieutenant [Johann Friedrich] von Sichart of our regiments had received their discharges, at their requests. The rebels were offered peace with very favorable terms. Therefore commissioners were sent from England to carry out the negotiations. Reportedly they are not pleased with this offer, but want their independence. Who knows, however, what they will do, since they have not stated their position. I wish for peace with all my heart.

The 26th - I went on picket duty. It was a beautiful day.

The 27th - Our entire corps crossed the Schuylkill on patrol, but we did not encounter any enemy. (Recent detachments have been very strong, often 200 men. However, of all the times, we have only once met an enemy patrol, at night, from which we made a few captives and had only one Hessian lightly wounded.)

The 28th - We returned at ten o'clock. During the afternoon it rained very hard.

The 31st - Another patrol was sent out during the night.

The 1st of May - It returned without having encountered the enemy. They did capture a lone rebel dragoon.

The 4th - During the night another detachment of 250 men went out. I was among them. We saw several of the rebel's light cavalrymen. We marched nine miles.

The 5th - The heat was so very great that several jaegers, who were sick to their stomachs, had to be sent back. We returned at twelve o'clock. Four of the Hessians were missing. The soldiers desert in large numbers. This happens with every patrol.

The 9th - Thoughts of peace have disappeared. Everyone speaks of war and great changes. France and Spain have joined together and declared war on England. How great the longing is to see our fatherland again this year, +++[5] I wish, but very much doubt, that things will change for us.

The 10th - I went on picket duty.

The 11th - I was relieved. During the night, at one o'clock, the entire corps was sent on patrol.

The 12th - At eleven o'clock we returned.

The 14th - We received orders that all the baggage, which we did not wish to take to the field, was to be packed ready to be taken aboard ship.

The 15th - It was a very warm day. Various ideas were held as to what was happening. Some thought we would go to Boston; others the West Indies; some even Europe, but no one knows. I will not even state my thoughts. I hope for the best, but will remain cautious. During the night I was included in a command which marched to the ferry boat at twelve o'clock. I was detached to a point two miles beyond to pick up a family.

The 16th - I returned at two o'clock in the afternoon. The heat was very great.

The 19th - I went on picket duty. During the evening a detachment of jaegers marched to Germantown.

The 20th - The rest of the jaegers [marched] early in the morning and also many of the army. A corps of about 5,000 rebels under the command of [Maria Joseph] Marquis de Lafayette had approached. Our troops marched, as far as Chestnut Hill, to meet him. As soon as he heard this, he retreated in great haste back across the Schuylkill. The English dragoons captured some French volunteers and cut down their major. Reportedly seventy prisoners were taken, but I did not see them. Four Indians were reported among them and 150 with the command.[6] I was not relieved from picket duty because the detachment did not return until evening.

The 21st - I was relieved at nine o'clock in the morning. It was very warm.

The 22nd - During the night I went out with a patrol but saw nothing. We went along the Lancaster Road and back along the Schuylkill.

The 23rd - We marched back again at ten o'clock and brought four deserters with us.

The 25th - It is said that we will soon leave Philadelphia for fear that the French fleet will blockade us here. It is certain that the ships with our baggage will sail today for New York and we will follow on land. Experience is the best teacher. We continue to work diligently on the defenses and if this report is true, it will give comfort to the enemy and our army must continue to exert itself. I hope for the best.

The 26th - Our Commanding General Howe departed today for England. General [Henry] Clinton took over the command.

The 28th - I went on picket duty.

The 29th - I was relieved.

The 30th - I went on patrol with a detachment commanded by the major. We saw no enemy.

The 31st - I received my first letter from Europe, but unfortunately none from my relatives.

The 1st of June - It was a very cold day with a heavy rain. Great preparations were made for our departure from Philadelphia. In two or three days we will surely depart.

The 7th - This morning the five [peace] commissioners, who are to negotiate with Congress, arrived from England. Generally speaking, the peace talks are not progressing as we would wish. God grant His blessing. I wish them to succeed. I went on picket duty. It rained very hard today.

The 8th - I was relieved as usual. During the night both of our regiments were embarked and we do not know where they are bound.[7] The separation makes me very sad. If we have to make a campaign it will be all the more unpleasant to be alone.

The 9th - Very beautiful weather. All our orders give us hope of marching soon.

The 10th - However, at two o'clock in the morning our entire corps went on patrol, but in vain, as usual.

The 13th - We hid in a woods where the rebels always pass. Some troops came along but because they saw us in time, our plan failed.

The 14th - After the prisoners were exchanged,[8] still others returned to the company today.

The 16th - At present there are not more than 6,000 men in the city. The army is already on the other side of the Delaware.

The 17th - At three o'clock this morning we were also carried across to Jersey. The heat was terrible. We marched to Haddonfield, seven English miles. On the way not more than eight rebels were seen, who were fired upon. During the evening our pickets made several reconnaissance patrols.

The 18th - We marched at ten o'clock, in the most unbearable heat, toward Waterford Township and Eayrestown,[9] eight miles. Our advance guard skirmished constantly with the enemy.

The 19th - We marched at three o'clock in the morning to Eayrestown, nine miles. It was like yesterday. From time to time the rebels would hide in the thick woods and engage the advance guard, which resulted in a very good Hessian jaeger being killed and several severely wounded and captured. They had destroyed two bridges outside our camp. Therefore I was ordered out to cover the repairs and then remained overnight on picket duty with Captain Ewald. We were undisturbed.

The 20th - At seven o'clock the corps and the Rangers marched. However, we remained at the bridges until the army arrived, as it was eight miles behind us. General [Alexander] Leslie commanded us as well as his brigade. At nine o'clock we moved ahead three miles to Mount Holly where the entire army, under General Clinton, made camp. It was a rainy day.

The 21st - At ten o'clock the last of the army arrived. At one o'clock the jaegers had to move forward more than 2,000 yards and became the advance posts.

The 22nd - At four o'clock in the morning the detached corps marched under General Leslie, in order to cover the flank of the army. Near Black Horse we joined the army. The rebels have dismantled all the bridges, making the march very difficult for us. It was a rainy day.

The 23rd - At three o'clock in the morning we marched through Black Horse, Rising Sun, Bordentown, to Farbridge, in order to provide cover for the army again. The bridges were all destroyed. The enemy had built redoubts and trenches. We received the false report that these had been abandoned. Therefore we moved forward close to the camp and about six-thirty the enemy opened fire with small arms. Shortly thereafter he cannonaded us severely, but without causing any harm. God be praised! When it was dark we pulled back.

The 24th - At four o'clock in the morning we moved back toward Crosswicks where the army had just arrived. We were at once detached to cover the flank. The enemy exchanged fire with our advance guard but lost one captain and two privates. We accompanied the army to Allentown where we made camp.

The 25th - We marched again at six o'clock in the morning. We were the advance guard. Because the enemy was behind us, we halted at Allentown and I was detached with a platoon to cover a road. The rebels soon appeared, but a jaeger killed an officer. Shortly thereafter they engaged us closely, but after the rear guard reinforced us, they had to retreat. We went as far as Monmouth County, beyond Freehold Township. It was very warm. We were on a height and our fate is beyond description.

The 26th - At five o'clock we marched; as usual, the rear guard. The enemy had disturbed us during the night up until we marched. We went about twelve miles. The enemy harassed us the entire day. I led a patrol off to one side. The heat was terrible. It was an extremely tiring day. Would to God it is the last one. The place where we halted is called Upper Freehold. During a marauding expedition the corps lost twenty men, but not one from the company.

The 27th - A day of rest, which was very necessary. The heat was terrible. I took a patrol about a mile but saw nothing. The enemy attacked all the army's pickets. I was really sick from the heat.

The 28th - At two o'clock in the morning we marched. We were the rear guard for General Knyphausen's column. As this was the first and had nothing to fear, we were thus spared from fatigue. The second, under the command of General Cornwallis, followed us with the Light Infantry as its rear guard, and the Queen's Rangers covering the flank. They were attacked at once and the major wounded. Between nine and ten o'clock the enemy came in large numbers. Cornwallis had already passed Freehold. The Light Infantry formed a front, but as they were too weak for this, they were reinforced immediately by the entire column. This consisted of the 1st and 2nd Brigades, English and Hessian Grenadiers, the Guards, the Rangers, and the 16th Dragoon Regiment. We did not think the enemy was strong, but finally discovered that this was Washington with his army. The cannonade was heavy by both sides and continued until four o'clock. However, our Britons again proved their bravery, suffering a loss of 400 to 500 men killed and wounded. The enemy was defeated and pursued as far as a swamp, unknown to us, where we took the greatest losses, which may have been the enemy's plan. However, it failed. Reportedly the rebel losses were more than 800 men. They retreated and our army followed slowly during the night. The heat was terrible and our greatest losses were the deaths due to the heat. Our column marched all night.[10]

The 29th - At five o'clock in the morning we halted three miles from Middletown. I went on picket duty at four o'clock in the afternoon. Everything was quiet by us but the English were much disturbed.

The 30th - At four o'clock in the morning we broke camp. Our march was very short, only to Middletown. We could see Sandy Hook. It was extremely hot. At night we left our camp and moved forward three miles, closer to the water.

The 1st of July - An enemy patrol approached but did not make contact.

The 2nd and 3rd - Everything was quiet. It rained hard, without letup.

The 4th - It was still the same.

The 5th - The weather was better but very warm. We marched at five o'clock in the morning and arrived at Sandy Hook at one o'clock. We remained lying there overnight.

The 6th - At seven o'clock we embarked and at twelve o'clock sailed with a favorable wind. We arrived in York at five o'clock. The ship was called *Fortitude*. In addition to our company, Captain [Friedrich Heinrich] Lorey's Company is also on board.

The 7th - We landed at eleven o'clock and marched eight miles to Harlem in extreme heat. Today I received my first letters, praise God! from my mother.

The 8th - I was sick.

The 9th - I was much better. Today Captain [Christoph Friedrich Joseph] von Waldenfels was assigned to us.

The 10th - I was sent with several jaegers down the East River to Long Island to send the heavy baggage to York. Our regiments lay at anchor there and are to go to Vlaatisland.[11]

The 11th - Please God, send us to Germany. The entire army is dissatisfied and does not wish to go to New England, as is expected. The French warships are reportedly outside the harbor.

The 12th - At noon Captain von Cramon turned the company over to Captain von Waldenfels.

The 13th - I went on picket duty.

The 14th - Everything remained quiet and I was relieved as usual.

The 15th - I went to New York. The city is rather long. Most of the houses are bad and small. The streets are irregular and bumpy. In a word, it did not please me.[12] On one side is the North River and on the other the East River.

The 16th - We marched at seven o'clock, about six miles, to the redoubt on Spitting Devil (in German,[13] because the hill is so high that one can speak to the devil.) This is the point where York province begins. All the heights have redoubts, forts, or blockhouses. We are very secure. The enemy can not attack us without suffering heavy losses. However, we are not here as defenders, but rather to attack, but the French fleet still lies near Sandy Hook. God grant that they will be defeated, otherwise we are lost.

The 17th - It was very warm. Our soil is bare rocks and sand, a poor camp. I will always hate this life. God grant me help soon.

The 25th - I went on picket duty.

The 26th - Relieved. It rained hard during the previous night.

The 29th - I received two letters from my sister, which were very old, however. The French fleet left our harbor and according to rumor an English fleet is just outside with many provisions. I wish with all my heart that this is true.

The 1st [of August] - The entire corps went on patrol as far as Philipse's house. There was a thick fog and we could not see twenty yards ahead. Because we had daily gone out with twenty or thirty men, the rebels were alert. Therefore they allowed our advance guard to pass, thinking it was our whole force. However, as the corps then followed, they fired, killed the horse of a mounted jaeger, and then fled. We marched, but as we could see nothing and assumed them to be a strong detachment, which could easily come from our rear, we pulled back.

The 2nd - I went on picket duty. The mosquitos bite dreadfully. It is a small torture. By the next day I was completely sore. During the evening the reserve picket went on patrol and reported to me that the rebels were very near me. Later reconnaissance proved this to be false.

The 3rd - A fire was set during the early morning in New York and seventy houses were burned down. Some disgruntled rebels were arrested.

The 4th - There was a violent thunderstorm such as on the previous days. A sloop near York was struck, blowing it up. One catastrophe after the other. The English fleet is not here, only a few provisions ships, and desertion from the army is rampant.

The 5th - A very warm day. We hardly know how to put up with it.

The 9th - I went on picket duty. During the evening a patrol reported to me that the enemy had taken position before our line. After this was checked out, however, it proved to be false. We had a frightful wind.

The 15th - It was rumored that the French fleet had attacked Rhode Island, but as two ships-of-the-line ran aground, and the English fleet had arrived, the French had sailed out to sea. Lord Howe followed them. We continued to have the terrible wind, which never letup.

The 18th - I went on picket duty. Everything remained quiet. We made frequent patrols. I sincerely believe that we will leave America this year, which is what the army wishes and hopes for. Additionally, it is my belief that we will go to New England. About the fleet which necessarily dictates our fate, we have disturbing news. A long wished-for English fleet has not arrived. We do not know what has happened to it. Pride and courage are very low. Apparently the English have need of their fleets in Europe. Would to Heaven I could make this war only in the newspapers in Europe. Then I would gladly participate.

The 21st - We had beautiful weather again early, after having had rain, wind, and storms for a long time.

The 29th - I went on picket duty. Everything was quiet.

The 30th - I was relieved. We hear very favorable reports from Rhode Island, but they have not been confirmed. This much is certain, the rebels launched an attack supported by the French.

The 31st - Today a patrol of 100 men went out to Philipsburg. The rebels fell on the rear and seven men are missing, including one man from our company, who was killed. All these people were in the rear guard. The patrol retreated quickly and they could not follow.

Suddenly the reports have changed. At three-thirty this afternoon the Rangers and Emmerich's Corps fought an engagement with the rebels. We got revenge. Both corps broke off contact. The rebels appeared with 300 men and attacked a small patrol which at once retreated, leading the rebels into an ambush where they were immediately counter-attacked by the cavalry and most of the Indians were cut down in the most gruesome manner. They probably lost sixty to seventy men, including several officers as well as the captain of the Indians. Our losses for the English amount to about twenty dead and wounded.

The 1st of September - Today I learned from ten deserters who came in that the jaeger whom I thought had been killed yesterday, was wounded and captured.

The 4th - The rebels have abandoned Rhode Island. General Clinton arrived two days too late. Our joy was not necessary.

The 8th - I went on picket duty and heard that our recruits had arrived at York.

The 10th - During the afternoon they arrived in our camp. There were 122 men, so-called jaegers, but handsome troops. I received letters at the same time, but they were old and had no bearing on my fate.

The 15th - I heard about the situation in Rhode Island, including that the French fleet had departed. At the same time the rebels retreated. Therefore they were attacked by our forces but had made very good disposition [of their troops]. Our regiments participated and lost seven dead, and our total losses were possibly 260 men. Currently it is very cold at night and not very warm during the day.

The 16th - Together with the Queen's Rangers we attacked the enemy outposts on the various roads early this morning, but things did not go as planned. We captured a total of 37 prisoners.

The 19th - I went on picket duty. We learned for certain that the enemy had retreated more than forty miles.

The 20th - I was relieved.

The 23rd - Our corps marched early in the morning, as far as the height beyond Philipsburg, where we halted. It rained hard day and night.

The 24th - The weather was better. General Knyphausen arrived at noon with the infantry. We moved forward another mile. The infantry occupied our ground so that the left wing rested on the North River, the right on the East River. The enemy was reportedly on Quaker Hill in the very far distance. There was a small garden beside the Philipse's house where I saw my first deer. It was white, almost as large as in Germany, but instead of antlers a more broad and flattened rack, and a similar manner of moving. In short, just like the German forest deer. We fired at several of them.

The 27th - Until this time we were undisturbed. I went on picket duty.

The 28th - I was relieved. During the morning we heard a heavy small arms fire from Jersey. Cornwallis had gone foraging there with the main army and General Gray was ordered against a large magazine which was protected by Lady Washington's Dragoon Regiment. The English Light Infantry attacked it and only six men survived; fifty were killed.

The 30th - I went on picket duty. Captain [Karl Moritz von] Donop made a patrol for six miles. The enemy had laid an ambush with 1,000 men with cannons. Our advance guard, which should have been farther ahead, was cut off. One lieutenant and two mounted jaegers were captured; seven foot jaegers and two mounted jaegers were killed, and one wounded. One [enemy] foot corporal, who was wounded, fell into our hands. Our company had no casualties. The lieutenant from the infantry escaped with fourteen men and rode through the open fields through the rebels.

The 1st of October - I was relieved, undisturbed, from picket duty. During the night, at nine-thirty, the corps went on patrol. We marched until five o'clock in the morning, fourteen miles, to the region of White Plains. Near Hammond's house we planned to establish a picket of twenty men. The Rangers and Emmerich's Corps had marched by a different route, and were to have joined us. However, during the night the rebels had moved their posts forward and the plan failed. As we withdrew they fired heavily against us from a distance.

The 2nd - At twelve o'clock we arrived in camp. I did not feel well.

The 3rd - Today I reported sick. I was suffering severe pain from dysentery. The rebels attacked at about ten o'clock against an infantry picket on our right. In the afternoon Major [Ernst Karl] von Prueschenck[14] and Captain von Wrede's Company had to go there to cover the regiment so that its rest would not be disturbed.

The 4th - It rained. The corps went on patrol. I was somewhat better.

The 9th - There was talk of marching. I reported myself as healthy.

The 10th - We marched back into camp at ten o'clock. It rained very hard. The rebels did not disturb us on the march.

The 11th - The same kind of weather.

The 12th - The weather improved, but was terribly cold. Toward noon a large enemy patrol approached. Because the non-commissioned officer's picket was drunk and not alert, it was fired upon. The cavalrymen drove the picket back. We feared they would enter the camp, they had approached so cleverly. They captured a double post which fired a salvo at them, slapped one of drunks in the face, and left him, taking only a horse.

The 14th - I went on a new picket, near where the enemy were.

The 15th - I was relieved, very quietly however, because the rebels were very close.

The 17th - Everything was quiet except for a patrol which I accompanied. We noticed a drastic change in the climate here as compared with Pennsylvania. It is already very cold, during the day, as well as at night.

The 18th - At nine o'clock in the morning the picket reported that some enemy had been seen. We had to move forward, head over heels, but saw nothing. Today it was very warm. The rebels are said to have sent back the new peace proposals. Some were burned and some thrown on the ground and walked on. Like many good things, unfortunately, it is not to be hoped for. Ten English and two Hessian regiments have orders to embark. Some say they are going to the

West Indies; others say one place and another; and all their guessing can be wrong.

The 21st - I went on picket duty. Everything was quiet.

The 22nd - I was relieved.

The 27th - Everything remains quiet. It is snowing but as the enemy desired to establish outposts quite close to us, our regiments, which were marching back and forth, saw them. There is talk of an expedition. The English Captain [Patrick] Ferguson was on the east coast of Jersey at Egg Harbor with 300 men and destroyed the ships, the harbor lumber facilities, and the stores there. When [Count Casimir] Pulaski heard this he advanced with 600 men, but the English went aboard ship. During the evening, however, a rebel officer by the name of Geliat,[15] who had previously served with the Hessians, deserted and pointed out how Pulaski could be attacked. Ferguson therefore landed, killed one colonel, two captains, and one lieutenant, and sixty men. I am not sure of the number of captives.

The 29th - Again today I went on picket duty. We have much work.

The 30th - As usual, I was relieved.

The 5th of November - I was once again ordered onto picket duty. It is already very cold. Would to God that we will soon enter winter quarters. We have had rain for several days, so everyone can understand, without a further description, our miserable situation.

The 8th - Beautiful weather but very cold. Our regiments are still embarked but no one knows for certain where they are to go. The army is becoming very weak. The enemy expresses no fear of us. We have many servants who are rebels and among ourselves I can not see what we can accomplish here with so few troops. To our proposed peace suggestions, the rebels have given no acceptable answer. They are approved by many who wish to serve the King. The enemy says we will return to Europe this winter. God grant it is so, but personally I believe we will never again see my fatherland.

The 11th - An astonishing wind.

The 12th - The weather was better. I went on picket duty.

The 13th - The corps marched out on patrol. The Rangers and Emmerich's Corps also went out, but by a different route. They attacked a rebel colonel, later capturing him and another colonel and killing two men and wounding two. Their losses were one dead and an officer and a private wounded. Our troops burned down several beautiful rebel buildings. They returned at five o'clock in the afternoon and I was relieved at six o'clock. During the night a dreadful rain and wind storm struck and many huts were knocked down.

The 14th - It continued to rain and was very cold.

The 15th - The order came to march. We were very pleased. We have yet to learn why.

The 16th - We left our corps at seven o'clock in the morning and arrived at Hellgate Ferry at noon. We were carried across and remained in quarters overnight. -- Something comical, my landlady did not want to put me up. She did not believe me to be an officer. I was thus embarrassed before the girls in the house.

The 17th - We marched at seven o'clock in the morning and arrived at Flushing on Long Island at noon. This city consists of about forty houses, most of which are very bad. On the left is the land side which seems rather narrow. My quarters are very bad, certainly not officer quarters. The window has only three panes which are not broken. The wind comes in everywhere and I have no firewood, but will try to get some tonight. Our company is in two barns. The troops must lie there close to one another and have no wood, either, and are not permitted to take any. The captain took over command of our new troops today. They were allocated [among the units] today. Lieutenants [Friedrich Ernst, Baron] von Reitzenstein and [Christian Friedrich] Bartholomai were assigned to us.[16] This causes me additional problems.

The 18th - I could not go to sleep well last night. My host is an English-American who owns many pigs, which were camped outside my window. They made a terrible noise all night. There were also five cows with them. The yard is very small. When I went out the door I had to wade through manure up to my knees. We are no longer to receive forage. I must sell my horse. Everyone is annoyed just as I am. I have no wood, except for what I have stolen.

The 29th - Our duty is not strenuous. No officers go on picket duty, but the jaegers must work all the harder because they received no quarters in houses. Therefore, they have to build huts. This makes a lot of work and the troops have many reasons to complain. Additionally, there is no wood nor building materials. It is rather cold and this is very hard on the men. If I were to enter all the rumors here, which are spread about, it would amount to only lies. Currently it is said that we will return to Europe in two months. Would to Heaven it were true. However, the English peace commissioners have left and the last favorable terms offered to the rebels were not accepted. Therefore, we can certainly not assume it will happen. Instead we will have another difficult campaign. The jaegers shoot many owls, a sort of quail which sits in trees, and a sort of rabbit which is not as large as the European rabbit; also a kind of mountain cock. There are a great many of all these in America. Today is a rainy day and I have the supervision of the hut construction.

The 18th of December - Our huts are still not ready. It appears first that the hard rain and bad weather has begun and second that the rain has penetrated all our hard work. The water stood above our shoes in the huts and the army had to move out of the huts because it rained harder inside than under the open sky. Now each one must be covered with reeds and straw. The troops are unhappy about that. The weather is good today, but yesterday it rained hard. True, the weather is cold, but last year at Philadelphia we had snow and cold weather at this time.

The 24th - A very heavy snow after having had the most beautiful weather the day before.

The 25th - A frightful storm and cold. Only with great difficulty could I get out of my quarters. It was very fortunate for the men that the huts were finished. Still the storm blew the snow in terribly so that in some huts the snow was two feet deep.

The 26th - Still the same weather. I can not remember having had such in Germany more than once. The cold increases and I recant what I wrote. It is colder than in Pennsylvania.

The 27th - A beautiful day but even colder. I must spend much time in my room.

The 28th - Still just as pretty and just as cold as previously. In many places the snow lies twelve feet deep.

The 30th - The cold continues. I have never seen it like this in America. The Sound[17] is almost completely frozen and we must make ourselves secure from an attack by the rebels. This is being done. However, it is rumored that our provisions are exhausted. That would be a great misfortune, but during the winter, time is passed with such stories. Such as now it is said for certain, and mentioned in the newspapers, that 25,000 Russians are coming. The transport ships have already gone to Riga from England to pick them up. If Heaven grants it, it will be a pleasant sight for me, certainly the most enjoyable in America.

1779

The 1st of January - Praise Heaven another [year] has begun and the last one survived, despite many crises. Heaven protect me in this year also. Do not treat me according to my deserts, but allow me to return to my fatherland this year. Then I will praise and never forget You.

There is no longer any bread or flour. Therefore the troops receive oatmeal which does not thrill them and with which they can make nothing. The provisions fleet did not leave England until October. If everything goes well, it could still be a long time in arriving and we still long for bread.

The 5th - Again today it is especially cold. The snow has melted together somewhat, but we will certainly get more.

The 9th - Today the weather changed. It rained all day and has been nice since. The cost of living has increased sharply and for a lot of money nothing is to be had. It is especially true with bread. The common soldier has it the worst. His pay is not sufficient to buy bread. Complaints are heard daily and it is necessary to feel sorry for the men. The frequent crimes which occur create problems for us officers. The jaegers steal and slaughter their landlords' cattle at night. Such complaints arise daily. We check them out every day but to no avail. Reportedly two provisions ships arrived in New York yesterday and the fleet has anchored at Sandy Hook. Heaven grant that this is not just a rumor. We do not know how to appreciate our good fortune. Supposedly our regiments in Rhode Island have it even worse. Except for their provisions they can buy nothing fresh. Furthermore, they do not even have a tree, nor a piece of firewood. How happy they will be when the weather improves and turns mild.

The 11th - It is confirmed concerning the fleet. Still some say it was only a few ships, which the rebels have captured. It snowed again and became very cold.

The 26th - The weather has changed completely. For a very long time and continuously it was cold. A packet boat from Germany arrived in York yesterday. I impatiently await for letters. We hear from South Carolina that General [James] Grant has made good progress. The Indians under the leadership of [John] Butler have created great fear among the rebels. Even the people of Philadelphia are starting to tremble.

The 5th of February - Lieutenant [Johann] Beck, who arrived about twelve days ago with reinforcements, came to York on leave and did not report back at the end of his leave. Therefore he is being sought everywhere. Our first reports were that a boat had been damaged and sunk opposite York at Brooklyn Ferry by the ice breaking up and that everyone had drowned. However, today we had the unpleasant report from Lieutenant Colonel [Andreas] Emmerich that Beck had been with him, in disguise, passed himself off as a private person, and enlisted in Emmerich's Dragoons. The next day, however, Beck came to him and confessed that he was an officer in our service. However, this did not help him. He was released from our service and was to have sought his fortune as one of Colonel Emmerich's men. This individual at once transferred him back to us and as this no longer satisfied him, he was to have his discharge. He wished to return as on officer but we have no further reports. We can believe nothing other than that he has gone over to the rebels. We have the embarrassment that an officer has deserted, although we have lost nothing in the individual. However, would to Heaven that it had occurred somewhere else.

The 12th - Beautiful weather. We have the most beautiful spring days. General Grant has captured the French island of St. Lucia in the West Indies. The French fleet is reportedly blockaded by ours at Martinique. Colonel [Archibald] Campbell has taken Georgia with the 71st Regiment and two Hessian battalions. The rebels have lost a great deal and 453 persons have been taken. They are brought into the York prison daily. It is reported that France has offered England peace. How much of all of this is to be believed, we can only wait and see.

The 23rd - A very changeable weather; first the most beautiful summer day, followed by extreme cold and storm. The Hessian Lieutenant Montluisant received his discharge. He was to be taken to England at no charge on a frigate. However, he went to the outposts and planned to go over to the rebels. He was forcibly arrested and brought to the provost in York. What is happening now to the officers? It appears we are losing our honor and I almost believe it has already disappeared. A packet arrived, however, without mail.

The 3rd of March - As I have recorded my most noteworthy daily activities here, I can not fail to note follies. Love has caught me in her net here in America, also. The personality of my good friend has once again awakened my life. Although this individual is not especially beautiful, nevertheless her understanding, if I were not +++ bashful and also frivolous person caught in her net. I am in love with everything about her +++ think she is beautiful. However, I am also too weak to express my feelings. All the fruit which I hope to have from this harvest +++ will consist of only looking, and the father and mother, who love their daughter more than I, from all appearances, will not be disappointed. A few minutes to be alone with her, the happier you are B+++ and it is just as good for me. I can make the following suggestion +++ and good +++ Germany, you are forgotten. We have very beautiful, warm weather. Several English regiments went to Elizabethtown in Jersey under the command of Colonel [Thomas] Stirling. They burned several enemy magazines and houses and brought back 22 prisoners. Several gentlemen of the Congress, who were staying there, barely escaped. General [William] Tryon went with English and Hessian troops to Horse Neck, destroyed some magazines, and captured three cannons and forty prisoners. However, as the rebels were much stronger than we were, the captured cannons had to be abandoned, but were spiked. A large amount of livestock was brought off, however.

The 13th - It snowed heavily and was rather cold.

The 14th - We had very stormy weather. February was much more pleasant and warmer than this month.

The 20th - We have continued to have very cold weather. Last night it was as cold as in winter. There is still snow on the ground and it does not go away. At Whitestone Ferry, a mile from here on the Sound, there are several transport ships with flatboats. They arrived several days ago. Because it is very near us, we expect to be embarked on them in order to undertake an expedition.

The 26th - More snow fell. It was very blustery weather.

The 28th - We heard that a fleet has arrived from England with uniforms for the [Ansbach-Bayreuth] Regiments and for us [Jaegers]. Therefore I went to New York, but they could not be disembarked.

The 7th of April - The weather is better now, but still very changeable. Yesterday it was frightfully warm and today a north wind makes it very cold and unpleasant. From Georgia we hear that the entire province has given in to the King, and the troops under the command of General [Augustine] Prevost have behaved well. The rebels lost 1,600 men, seven cannons, and all their baggage in a battle.

The 17th - Today we have rain, but otherwise we have had the warmest summer days, nearly as warm as in Germany during the dog days. From the West Indies we hear that the French Admiral [Charles Hector] Comte d'Estaing had been blockaded at Martinique by our Admiral [John] Byron. Because the provisions were short, he found it necessary to give battle, which he then lost. As they say, we are awaiting confirmation and details. There is much talk of peace, but it will probably be just like last year.

The 10th of May - With much certainty reports, even in the newspapers, were made concerning the recent sea battle. In the end I find that they were all untrue, as nothing noteworthy has taken place, but the newspapers must also find some fictitious thing, so that they have something to occupy their pages. Three days ago 3,000 men were embarked and sailed under the command of General [Edward] Mathew. No one knows where.

The 18th - Without warning, the order came to get wagon horses and to prepare the heavy baggage for moving, in order to send it on its way on the shortest notice. Most of the troops have already moved out of their quarters and some have gone to York Island.

The 19th - As our army does not have the strength nor capability to take the field, I can not understand where it can go. It is either to fool the enemy until the reinforcements come from England, or we will move up the North River, which we will surely do. Reportedly a strong fleet is coming from England. There are also reports of a successful battle in Georgia. Certainly 20,000 men would eliminate all our problems. Then we could leave America with honor. However, the rebels will surely not allow England to do this.

The 28th - The troops under General Mathew's command have landed in Virginia at the entrance to the Chesapeake Bay and captured a large number of ships and magazines from the rebels. We finally received the order to march tomorrow and therefore our peaceful winter quarters will come to an end. We can anticipate much fatigue and unrest. How happy I would be if this were our last campaign. However, I will have patience and give myself over to the higher will and to Him, who has protected me during two campaigns and other great perils. It is a small favor to protect me in a third one, and I can undertake it with more peace of mind if I do not disturb myself with too much nonsense and forget the things on which I tend to dwell. We are such wretched people; and me in particular+++

The 29th - We left Flushing at three o'clock in the morning. We marched to Lawrence Neck and embarked in flatboats, together with the English Grenadiers. We crossed the Sound to York province, and as soon as we were on land, marched through West Chester to Cortlandt's house, beyond Philipse's, and on to Philipse's Manor, sixteen miles, where we had camped last fall. Even today I can recall the great heat which I had forgotten in my peaceful quarters. Heaven protect me during this campaign, and I hope to recover during the coming winter, when I will certainly not again commit such folly as in Flushing. I went on picket duty. It was very quiet. We did not know where the enemy was situated.

The 30th - It rained a bit. Suddenly at one o'clock a patrol of 300 men under the command of Major Prueschenck was sent out. Other officers included Captains Ewald, Lorey, and Waldenfels and Lieutenants Ebenauer, [Maximillian] Cornelius, and me. We embarked on transport ships at Philipse's Ferry. We found Hessians, who had just arrived from Virginia already on board. We had 600 men on board. We lay there until three o'clock, when the anchor was raised, and we sailed up the North River.

The 31st - The fleet anchored at eleven o'clock at Tellar's Point and we debarked at twelve o'clock under the command of General [John] Vaughan. Unexpectedly I saw many troops, who were the elite of the army, about 2,000 men. **Note** - They had just returned from an expedition to Virginia, the English Grenadiers, the Light Infantry, the 33rd Regiment, the Legion, Ferguson's, three battalions of Hessian Grenadiers, and Robertson and 200 jaegers. We marched three miles to the right with the 33rd Regiment and the Hessian Grenadiers and occupied a high hill. The others cut off Verplanck's Neck. I went on picket duty. A corps of rebels was eight miles from us but everything remained quiet. One hundred jaegers and the 17th, 63rd, and 64th Regiments were landed on the Jersey shore, opposite, and not far away from us at Haberstraw, where the enemy had several batteries. Those which were on Stony Point were captured when the enemy abandoned them after setting them on fire. We then set up a battery there, and with the help of some row galleys, opened fire on the rebel Fort

Lafayette on Verplanck's Point. Next a frigate and a row galley passed the fort in order to cut communications to the north.

The 1st of June - The cannonade commenced at daybreak and at noon the garrison surrendered. Four officers and 71 men were in the garrison. A battery was nearby. It was small but masterfully and well-fortified, but the entire armament was only three cannons. If they had 200 men and more courage and artillery, they could have made it very difficult for us. Shortly thereafter a very good uniform with a silk lining was found, and nearby the body. Both were found hidden. The prisoners disclaimed any knowledge. We were told that possibly it had been a high ranking Frenchman. About two o'clock we marched three miles farther and into camp at Herecland's Creek, two miles from Peekskill.

The 2nd - I went on picket duty. A cavalry patrol was observed by our outposts. At five o'clock in the evening we moved back a half-mile to a better post, which we maintained, near a bridge.

The 3rd - At eight o'clock in the morning our army marched through Peekskill to a creek about three miles beyond. We met several dragoons and skirmished with them. We suffered no losses, but the enemy did. We learned later that a colonel was killed. I have never seen such plundering as on this march. The troops had permission to do so and Heaven help the house which a jaeger entered.

The 4th - I went on picket duty and everything remained quiet today, which pleased me.

The 5th - A rebel boat came down the North River and shot a sentry from the Legion, fired heavily into our camp,. and spread a great alarm among us. Shortly thereafter it approached land near our outpost and as it did not withdraw, our major took 100 men and forced it back. The engagement was very sharp, but our loss very small. Our company had no more than one man lightly wounded. The enemy, which numbered 400 men, had to retire beyond Peekskill.

The 6th - My picket was very peaceful. During the evening I was reinforced by one officer and twenty men from the Legion who were to support me with bayonets in an emergency.

The 7th - We laid an ambush before our outposts. The rebels approached and a non-commissioned officer from our company, who had demonstrated his bravery on previous occasions, became too excited this time, captured two prisoners, one of whom he seriously wounded.

The 8th - I went on picket duty. Our tour of duty was very strenuous. I wanted to pull back, but who would not do everything possible under the orders of such a fine major.[1] We laid an ambush again, the enemy approached, but we could not fire more than two shots, although well-directed, according to what we were told later. During the evening an officer and thirty Hessian grenadiers joined us, as a reinforcement instead of the English.

The 9th - Everything is quiet but the heat is nearly unbearable.

The 10th - I had a peaceful picket.

The 11th - It was still quiet. The heat is terrible and our duties strenuous. Lieutenant Cornelius and 100 men were detached to Stony Point under the command of Captain Lorey. Therefore I go on picket duty every other day.

The 12th - I went on picket duty. The grenadiers joined us as previously. This evening Lieutenant [Johann Heinrich] Wolff arrived as a reinforcement.

The 13th - It rained very hard today. Fortunately we had some very well-built huts made of boards.

The 14th - Today we had many thunderstorms and rain, which continued during the night. Fort Lafayette was improved with several trenches and three block houses. The Jersey shore was considerably fortified and can be placed under water.[2] There is certainly a possibility that the rebels can recapture it.

The 15th - I went on picket duty. My health was not the best. The weather was very good again.

The 16th - Good weather, not so warm. At twelve o'clock a dragoon patrol ran into an ambush but was not captured. However, two horses were fatally wounded. If Heaven could only get me out of America, but things do not go as I would wish. I must remember the real reason of our discontent. This fate is certainly very cruel for those who think as I do +++ Lord, how much I must put up with here!

The 17th - Rainy weather. The longer we remain here the more unpleasant this camp seems to me. I have no good friend to speak with, my health is not good, the region is completely wild, bare cliffs and unpleasant. I never remember such a miserable camp. How cruel fate has been, and does not seem to change.

The 18th - I went on picket duty. Everything was quiet. During the evening I pulled back across the bridge. The corporal established a position. During the night the watch sounded an alarm. They fired a great deal. We believed the enemy actually planned an attack.

The 19th - A quiet day. To my great disgust there was talk of marching.

The 21st - I went on picket duty. Everything was quiet.

The 23rd - The heat is extremely bad. No one knows how to stay cool.

The 24th - I went on picket duty. Nothing was seen of the enemy.

The 25th - At four-thirty in the afternoon we had a heavy thunderstorm and rain. It struck three men in the Hessian grenadier camp, but did not kill them. One recovered at once, but the third one was seriously injured.

The 26th - There is talk of news which I am almost afraid to enter here. It is reported that General Prevost, who commands in South Carolina, was defeated, captured, and annihilated during the attack on Charleston, just like Burgoyne. God grant that this is not true, otherwise we dare not hope for peace. Work on the fortifications is continuing and everything is being done well.

The 27th - I went on picket duty. We received the order to march. At eight-thirty we moved out and at ten o'clock embarked on the ship *Caledonia* near Fort Lafayette. At two o'clock we sailed back down the North River with the ebb tide, but with a contrary wind. The troops from Jersey and the jaegers were embarked with us. A garrison of 1,500 remained there.

The 28th - We sailed at three-thirty in the morning with a contrary wind. It rained very hard. Yesterday we collided with another ship and I was nearly on no ship, if I had not been a fatalist. At ten o'clock we anchored. We sailed with a favorable wind at one-thirty and by three-thirty we were already near Philipse's house, where we anchored. An order which we received led us to think that we would continue down [river]. However, this changed everything +++ unfortunately, and the gentlemen, from pride, came one after the other.[3] At nine o'clock we received the order to disembark and we entered camp at twelve o'clock.

The 2nd of July - I went on picket duty. At daybreak we went on patrol with the English but did not know where we were going.

The 3rd - During the past night our mounted jaegers returned. They had ridden out forty miles and had planned to attack a rebel cavalry regiment "Chelton". However, shortly before they arrived at their goal, the English made a wrong turn, giving the rebels time to escape and only eight dragoons were captured. However, many saddles, sabers, and equipment were seized. The English had one man killed. The Jaegers lost an officer's horse during the continuous attacks by the militia on the return. However, some of them [the militia] were captured.

The 5th - Everything remains quiet and a great heat causes us discomfort. **Note** - On the 1st I had proposed that my command be strengthened. However, because I often had disagreements with my captain, I again failed. I will be glad to get a heavy load off my back. It seems good friends are the instigators of our discord. I am well aware, however, a certain politic tells me to be quiet, and I always learn more from listening to such people. But I will say nothing more in order not to incite them more.

The 8th - On the third I forgot to note that three regiments arrived in the Sound from Rhode Island. Lieutenant [Alexander Wilhelm] Bickel and forty jaegers from our troops were then embarked with them. They again sailed out of the Sound, under the command of General Tryon, but we do not know where they are going. We received the report today that our right wing, consisting of the Light Infantry, English Grenadiers, three battalions of Hessian grenadiers, and the Queen's Rangers, under General Vaughan, has moved forward.

The 10th - I went on picket duty. Everything was quiet.

The 11th - We had an astonishing rain.

The 13th - I received news of General Tryon's expedition. He landed at New Haven, burned enemy stores, sixteen ships, and several houses and captured three cannons. In so doing we lost three men. A seventy-year-old man was stoned to death by twenty English soldiers because he railed at and cursed us. The rebels carry their wickedness to such extremes. No one believes that such barbarity can be expected from them. Fairfield consisted of 300 houses and was burned down because the inhabitants killed an artillery guard. The troops then embarked again and the fleet continued up the Sound, but we do not know where it is going. The reports concerning General Prevost were unfounded. He is on Johnson Island, eight miles from Charleston, awaiting reinforcements. Also, he can do nothing more because of the great heat.

The 16th - About two o'clock this morning we heard several cannon shots on the North River. At five o'clock they were quite near us. It was signaling between ships but they signified nothing good. At first we thought the enemy was marching against us and therefore made preparations to meet them. During the afternoon, however, we received the sad news which made us especially downcast. During the night the rebels had attacked and captured the newly-established Fort Stony Point. We received orders to be ready to march.

The 17th - We hear so many falsehoods and rumors that it discourages me from making entries here.

The 18th - At daybreak we marched with the entire army as far as Tops Ferry, three miles, where the army camped. We marched a mile to the right and camped on the flank. We had a very secure camp on Saw Mill Creek.[4] Today we learned more about the surprise at Stony Point. The enemy planned to attack only the pickets and, because they heard that the pickets were always in a poor state of readiness, this happened and was successfully executed, without a shot being fired. The enemy took advantage of this opportunity and continued on, taking the fort without the least resistance and without loss. Colonel [Henry] Johnson was the commandant; the 17th Regiment, two companies of grenadiers, and 100 men of Robinson's Regiment made up the garrison. Of this number, thirty were killed with bayonets, fifty wounded, and 250 taken prisoner. The others fled into the countryside. In their defense, the English say that the rebels made the attack from the water. Be that as it may, they were not alert. Today our four regiments went aboard ship in order to relieve the fort at Verplanck's Point and to recapture the other. Our march was for the same purpose, or at least to threaten the enemy.

The 19th - After the enemy had heavily cannonaded and bombarded our Fort Lafayette, they saw our troops arriving aboard ship. They were at once discouraged and called up a row galley. Forty cannons from the fort and four mortars, as well as their own cannons, were directed against us. As they say, Fort Lafayette was not such an easy conquest. The commander of the fort fired upon them in a frightful manner and sank the rebel ship with all its cannons. The rebels abandoned the position. Our troops took possession [of the sunken ship] without any resistance and recovered the cannons from the water, because the water is not deep there. The ship's masts are fully visible. **Note** - On 17 July General Tryon returned from his expedition, and this afternoon Lieutenant Bickel also returned. They had burned many stores in New Haven. Norwalk suffered the same fate, but the English took very few prisoners. They killed everyone. Many will call this terrible, but anyone who knows the rules and customs of war will say with me, this is the way to end the war.

The 20th - I went on picket duty but first the corps had marched four miles to allow the army to collect forage. At daybreak it rained very hard but this did not last longer than one hour. At ten o'clock I moved my picket and at one o'clock the Queen's Rangers, Light Infantry, and the 17th Dragoons moved past and entered camp on the other side of Saw Mill Creek. At two o'clock I also moved across and joined their line of pickets.

The 21st - At six o'clock in the evening our camp also marched back. We entered our previous camp beyond Philipse's house on Hog Kill at one o'clock. It was extremely warm and the heat spoiled a good afternoon. General Cornwallis arrived from England and said that 10,000 troops had sailed ten days ahead of him, and therefore we await their arrival daily.

The 23rd - It rained all day. The Refugees brought in much livestock and also several prisoners. This made the rebel militia very nervous.

The 26th - It still continued to rain. Today one officer and fourteen privates, deserters from Colonel [Charles Tuffin] Armand's Corps, arrived. They were all Germans and part of them had been brought to Boston in ships and part had been captured with Burgoyne.

The 29th - I went on picket duty. It rained very hard. Yesterday and this morning we received orders to march, but shortly before daybreak they were cancelled. Reportedly we are to go back, but where we will go then, no one knows. Today we received the news that the rebels in Carolina had attacked Prevost's outposts near Stono Ferry and been beaten back with the loss of 300 men, according to rumor.

The 30th - At three o'clock in the morning 150 infantry and our cavalry made a patrol as far as Tarrytown. Our cavalry clashed with sixty dragoons who had already skirmished with Emmerich, from whom they had made six captives. Our jaegers joined in , however, and recaptured the prisoners and one rebel, who due to misunderstanding was severely wounded. Four rebels were killed on the spot. We lost one horse.

The 31st - At five o'clock in the morning we marched. The entire army returned to York Island and we reentered our previous camp of last year, at Spitting Devil. We arrived at nine o'clock. The woods and trees have all been cut down, therefore it was very difficult for our troops to build huts, and our company made camp with their wool blankets.

The 1st of August - Many various opinions are held concerning our return. Rumor is that a French fleet is expected here. Again, that Comte d'Estaing had sneaked past Admiral Byron at Martinique. Therefore, it is assumed that he [d'Estaing] might come again to Sandy Hook. Certainly no one knows the truth. We have had eight days of rainy weather already and it has been very cold.

The 3rd - Very cold, rainy weather. The number of our sick has greatly increased, especially, however, I believe they make themselves sick by eating unripe fruit, which is considered very unhealthy. A newspaper reports that Byron has defeated d'Estaing +++ if it is true, I will record the details.

The 4th - I went on picket duty. It was astonishingly hot. News from St. Eustatius, although no picket boat has arrived, is that the Comte d'Estaing, who has been reinforced by seven warships, eleven frigates, and 95 transports with troops, went to St. Vincent and Grenada with 27 ships-of-the-line, eleven frigates, and some troops, and captured those islands. Following this, Byron, with nineteen warships and five frigates, arrived and attacked the French. The battle lasted two and one-half hours. The French fleet was defeated and withdrew to Hispaniola.

The 5th - At daybreak we received news that the English Light Infantry planned to attack the enemy. They made their attack; our corps supported them, and chased the enemy a great distance, but to no avail. Our company had two men, apparently deserters, missing.

The 10th - I went on picket duty. Everything remained quiet, although an enemy corps was nearby. Last night a Hessian corporal deserted, as did two jaegers from our company. Things look bad for us on all sides. Rumor is that the English fleet in the West Indies has been defeated. No one knows for sure how it looks there.

The 11th - Early this morning our corps went on patrol in order to find the enemy, but they had pulled back. I was relieved at ten o'clock.

The 13th - Everything is quiet. It is astonishingly hot and oppressive. It puts me in a bad humor.

The 15th - I went on picket duty.

The 16th - During the afternoon we received a report that an enemy patrol had been seen near the Philipse's house and the corps hurried there. However, like every other time, we are either too late or have wrong information. It was like that again. The rebels were long gone. A corporal deserted from our company.

The 17th - News arrived that Byron had defeated the French fleet and four 40-gun ships had been captured.

The 18th - We began removing the cannons from the redoubts on this side of Kingsbridge. Reportedly all of these works will be destroyed. In their place, very strong forts will be laid out the other side of Kingsbridge. Supposedly when everything is ready, we will go to Long Island. +++

The 20th - I went on picket duty. It rained all day and all through the night.

The 24th - Once again we had good weather. On the nineteenth of this month the rebels had attacked Paulus Hook. After many of the garrison had been withdrawn, the rebels approached during the night. They captured a redoubt and spiked a cannon, but did not have time to accomplish anything more, because the fire from a small redoubt, in which there were Hessians, was so heavy against them. They did capture forty men, however, and lost one captain and six privates. One unfavorable incident after the other. It seems our situation is not the best. At noon the news arrived that a rebel patrol was near Philipse's house. We marched there but they had left two hours previously. When we arrived we were told that a large fleet commanded by Admiral [Marriot] Arbuthnot had arrived at Sandy Hook.

The 25th - I went on picket duty. The weather was good until evening when it began to rain. From midnight until two o'clock in the morning we heard a heavy cannonade from the direction of Sandy Hook.

The 26th - Reports about the fleet became more frequent. Supposedly three English regiments and English recruits, as well as recruits for our regiments, including thirty men for our company, a total of 3,000 men, have arrived. The second division, awaited momentarily, is reported to be bringing the remaining troops and the Hessian recruits.

The 30th - I went on picket duty. I was very sick. Everything remained quiet. I received good news in letters from Germany, but they also greatly embarrassed me. First, I received my promotion to captain and with it the question, did I wish to be recalled [to Germany]. Second, however, because of sickness and the fear I could not ask so much, although I very much wished to do so.

The 2nd of September - The rebel reports tell us much about [John] Butler, the commander of the Indians. They scalp and cause the rebels great fear, but it is believed, as a large corps has marched against them, that they will be brought under control. We have no good news from the West Indies.

The 3rd - I went on picket duty.

The 7th - On both pickets everything was quiet.

The 11th - The weather is rather cold; the north winds are especially raw. Desertions from the Hessian corps are very frequent.

The 11th [sic] - We have finally received news from Penobscot. George Collier, with an English fleet of seven ships, had blockaded the rebel fleet, which they themselves then set on fire. Six ships, including two frigates, were captured. The remaining fifty were burned. At the same time 500 to 600 rebels were lost during this attack.

The 12th - Very cold weather. I went on picket duty.

The 17th - Very warm weather during the day. Because we had reports of enemy movements, several patrols were sent out. Toward morning one encountered an English [patrol], which delivered a heavy fire. However, it caused no harm. We were alarmed several times today.

The 18th - The past night was very restless. Our patrols fired upon one another. The ships reported seeing heavy firing ahead of us, but I was relieved without having seen a rebel.

The 23rd - I went on picket duty.

The 24th - There were reports that the rebels planned to attack Morrisania, where the Refugees were camped. Therefore we marched at midnight. Five miles from our camp we laid an ambush, but the enemy did not come. At seven o'clock in the morning we returned.

The 25th - At eleven o'clock in the morning the Hessian recruits arrived, 224 men plus two officers.

The 26th - We had a terrible rain all day and all through the night.

The 27th - It changed but the wind was very strong.

The 28th - I went on picket duty.

The 29th - At seven o'clock in the morning Captain von Wangenheim, Lieutenant von Reitzenstein, and 100 men went on a command beyond Fort Knyphausen on the North River, because the enemy was expected to land there. This would place the general, who is at Monizen's house, in great danger. The Bose Regiment which was there had to move to York because it was too weak for duty. Everyone was sick and half of our army lay in the hospital.

The 1st of October - During the past night, at three o'clock, we were alarmed. The enemy attacked our outposts, but failing to accomplish anything, quickly pulled back. We remained under arms until daylight. It was very cold. Three deserters, who came over, told us that this Armand, at the urging of our previously deserted jaeger Corporal [Wilhelm] von Schonauer, had planned to attack us with his entire corps.

The 2nd - I went on picket duty. Other than a flag of truce which arrived, nothing changed.

The 3rd - A patrol of 100 men went out, including the Hussars and 24 infantrymen from the 64th Regiment. This detachment laid an ambush. Twenty-five light horse came up behind the Hussars and cut their way through. This resulted in numerous wounded on both sides. Next, they encountered the English who delivered a full volley. The lieutenant and trumpeteer lost their horses and fell into our hands. Many other horses and dragoons were wounded but escaped.

The 6th - I went on picket duty. It was very cold and rained steadily until ten o'clock at night. The winter wind will certainly arrive four weeks early this year, because the weather is not as changeable as last year, but it is certainly cold with a cruel wind.

The 8th - The same weather continues. I strongly wish to enter winter quarters. If we have not earned this, it is not our fault.

The 10th - I went on picket duty. This was a restless night because the outposts reported to me that they had heard something ahead of them. Although we had heard that the enemy planned to attack us, this did not happen.

The 12th - An hour before daylight the corps marched on patrol in several detachments, because the enemy swarmed about us in great numbers as if to attack Doris' house. Part went up the North River to Philipse's house; the cavalry on the road in that direction; and we crossed at Courtland's Bridge. Near Babcock's house we all came together without having seen a rebel. Their intelligence is so good that they know every movement that we make out of our camp. About six o'clock in the evening we had a very severe thunderstorm and rain.

The 14th - I went on picket duty, unaware however, that we had advanced and that the enemy was just opposite us, but everything remained quiet.

The 17th - Our sick become evermore numerous. It is one of the greatest stupidities of the army. Considering our situation, I do not know what I should say or think. Not far from The Narrows ships have been sunk to make it more difficult for the French fleet to enter the harbor. All the pilots are on board the admiral's ship and no ships are allowed to depart. The French fleet lost the West Indies and shortly it appeared on the coast of Georgia. The French have captured an English warship and a great storm scattered the enemy fleet, extensively damaging their ships and possibly occupying them for a long time before they can visit us. The 44th Regiment and the Knyphausen and Lossberg Regiments, which left here six weeks ago, encountered the most terrible storm ever. Two ships of their fleet fell into rebel hands, some returned here, and several are still missing, which either sank or are also in rebel hands. We have never had a period of such a time as this. God watch over the English at sea. This will place us in an even worse situation.

The 19th - I went on picket duty.

The 20th - There are reports today that the English fleet has arrived near Sandy Hook from the West Indies.

The 22nd - The fleet has again departed and reportedly they are looking for the French. They will surely find them in Georgia, as even the rebels say they have gone there and captured two ships of the line, eight frigates, and 2,000 land troops. Therefore, we have lost that province again. God grant that this is not true. One misfortune follows after another; our good times are over. Once again we have the nicest weather and during the day it is very warm.

The 23rd - I went on picket duty. It rained during the evening. We and our camp were alarmed by several shots heard by our outposts. Among others, one post called out, "Liva",[5] the word for an alarm, before they fired. Everyone claimed that the enemy was at hand, but it must have been only imagination, because none of the patrols sent out could find anything.

The 25th - Beautiful weather but a cold wind.

The 27th - I went on picket duty. Everything was quiet but the enemy approached and assembled at White Plains. The reason could be that the English have left Verplanck's Point and Stony Point and the rebels have free passage to act. These forts, which were of such importance to us, were abandoned without a fight. The garrison from Rhode Island has arrived at York, leaving that island, also We have conquered nothing, but lost a lot this year. Our winter quarters are to be behind Fort Knyphausen. Conditions are improving for us, but the news is worse every day.

The 30th - I went to New York to visit our regimental headquarters. I was very satisfied because our colonel was determined that I was to return to Europe, having received my recall

The 1st of November - I went on picket duty. Everything remained quiet. However, the worst thing is that our jaegers frequently desert, supposedly because of the poor winter quarters. There is no longer any wood and each day we must bring some here, which is for building huts, but was originally to have been used for firewood.

The 7th - At twelve o'clock today the corps received orders to march. I did not accompany it however, but left the company at ten o'clock and said goodbye to all my duties. I moved to New York until the fleet for Europe is ready to sail. God grant that it sails soon. How happy I am not to be forced to spend this year in the beautiful winter quarters where the jaegers will be. They are building huts for the winter, near the Morris house, two miles beyond Fort Knyphausen.

The 18th - By means of an express ship from St. Augustine, the report has arrived that Admiral Arbuthnot has announced the following reliable news. The French with 4,000 men and the rebels with 7,000 men stormed Savannah on 9 October. They were defeated with a loss of 3,000 men. The French have gone back on board their ships, and the latter have retreated to the Carolinas. They quarreled after the attack and it almost came to a battle. As for myself, I am still here awaiting orders to embark. God, who has brought me this far and seen me safely through three campaigns, will surely see me across the sea in good time and safely back to my fatherland. From what I hear, the jaegers are still forced to lie under the open skies despite the very cold weather. They must carry all the wood needed to built their huts, on their backs, for three miles.

The 19th - At five o'clock in the afternoon the garrison moved out to fire a *feu de joie*. The battalions were aligned in the following order: first the Scots, then four battalions of Hessian Grenadiers, and our two [Ansbach] battalions on the left wing. The front was toward the North River. When it was dark Fort George fired a 21-gun salute and then the garrison fired a running fire. Paulus Hook then answered in a similar manner. Fort George fired another 21-gun salute and the line fired as before, and then the same a third time, followed by everyone shouting hurrah. Supposedly a ship has arrived which has brought better news concerning the fleet.

The 26th - It snowed very hard today and the weather is exceptionally cold.

The 1st of December - My stay here is becoming a very long one but I must admit that if I must go to sea, I do not look forward to it. We are told daily of the good fortune not only of the West Indian fleet but also of the fleet in England. However, I can not confirm the reports until a ship arrives from those places.

The 2nd - We had a hard rain today and an astonishing thunderstorm during the evening. The orders which arrived today were to embark on the sixth.

The 5th - There was a terrible snowstorm all day and it turned very cold. I received a countermanding order concerning my embarkation. On the other hand an order was issued for 12,000 men to be ready to embark. Possibly we will sail part way with them.

The 8th - I rode out to visit the Jaegers and my good friends and to take my departure from +++ (foolishness) was quite grievous for me. It is still very cold.

The 11th - The order came to go aboard on the thirteenth. Today a ship arrived from the West Indies, from which we heard that it knew nothing of the French fleet. A ship also arrived from Savannah, which confirmed the victory over the French and rebels. The first lost 67 officers and 700 men, some say 1,000, and the latter 50 officers and 500 men.

The 13th - At ten o'clock in the morning we were ordered to embark. We waited on the Wood Wharf until eleven o'clock when a thick fog and rain forced cancellation of the orders. It was so dark that I could hardly find the city. I spent the afternoon and evening in the company of very good friends.

The 14th - By nine o'clock we were ready but because the wind was frightfully strong, we could not embark. I was very pleased to be able to have time with good friends prior to my departure.

The 15th - We went aboard ship at ten o'clock in the morning. I went with the last boat and, because the wind was against us, had to travel until one o'clock. Our ship is the *Charming Nancy*. In my entire life I have never been so cold as at this time. We brought a half-dead jaeger aboard ship with us. My transport consisted of Lieutenant [Adolf Daniel] von Strahlendorf, Regimental Surgeon [Andreas Friedrich] Pflug, and 45 men, invalids and those recalled. Our ship is well-equipped. God be with us to England.

The 16th - It was reported early that the badly frozen jaeger, [Johann Adam] Liebermann, died this morning at four o'clock. We still lay at anchor. There had been a heavy snow so that it was no longer so cold. Toward evening our dead companion, as usual, was sewn in a blanket filled with stones and thrown overboard.

The 17th - During the morning the Surgeon's Mate Burger died and as usual, at sundown, was thrown overboard. We sailed from five to six o'clock and anchored near Staten Island.

The 18th, 19th, and 20th - We had an astonishing storm. We had to remain at anchor. Our ship rolled considerably and we wished to sail onward.

The 21st - At nine o'clock the anchor was raised. The wind was from the southwest and not especially good for our departure. We anchored at one o'clock near Sandy Hook. The storm was strong and our ship rolled violently. What would it be like on the ocean?

The 22nd - I can not adequately describe our fleet; the appearance of 130 to 140 transport ships, including ten to twelve armed East Indiamen and a lone sloop with eighteen cannons. (Therefore our escort is weak.) The wind is very good, from the northwest, for our departure, but unfortunately we still lie at anchor. Toward evening our sailors brought four French seamen, captured on a warship, aboard and a German who had been an officer in Prussia and then for the rebels. He claimed to have deserted and come to New York. His name is Wolffen and he is treated as a prisoner by us.

The 23rd - The wind was from the north, the sea was calm, and at twelve-thirty we sailed, beginning our voyage in the Lord's name. The wind increased toward evening so that we sailed six miles in an hour and the sea still remained calm. During the night we lost sight of the American coast.

The 24th - A northwest wind, absolutely perfect. Every hour we sailed seven miles but the ship tossed about terribly because during the afternoon we had a strong wind.

The 25th - The wind from the northeast and therefore not as good as we would wish. It is very much like a storm. Lord abide with us. Early this morning we saw a sad sight. A two-masted ship had developed a leak during the night so that the water entered very quickly. It approached our ship. A merchant on that ship bound for Madeira transferred with his baggage to our ship. The captain from that ship was already alongside our ship. The sailors complained bitterly when they had to return to their ship and turn back to New York. Heaven protect them. It will soon sink. At twelve o'clock the storm began and by four o'clock it raged terribly. Our provisions and baggage, which had been protected and securely tied, tore loose. Even the doors caved-in. No one was sure of his life in the cabin. During the night it was frightful. I would like to forget this Christmas Day.

The 26th - At three o'clock in the morning the wind, which had blown so terribly, abated. However, the seas ran exceptionally high all day. Our ship was continuously thrown back and forth. The cracking noises were frightful. We still believed we were about to sink.

Nothing could be cooked, and we could see only six ships from our fleet.

The 27th - We had a good wind from the northwest, but our ship was still very unsteady. We were all miserable. All my limbs ached from trying to hold on in bed. Toward evening the wind increased and during the night we had another storm. A servant who wished to make our baggage more secure fell and lay dying for half an hour.

The 28th - The wind from the west and stormy. Our fleet now consisted on forty ships. It was impossible to cook.

The 29th - A storm out of the northwest and nothing could be cooked.

The 30th - A storm out of the northwest. We have lost all but two of the ships. We could not cook; a bad day and night, but good as an indication that Heaven protected us. I was very sick and our only consolation, we had sailed 900 miles Our forward mast had been damaged. Toward evening the wind and the sea became rather calm, but the ship still rolled rather violently.

The 31st - The wind from the southeast was rather weak and mild. I was still miserable. For a week it had been very warm and this evening we had another thunderstorm.

1780

The 1st of January - The wind from the northwest blew very strong and toward evening a storm came up. Every half hour we had rain or hail.

The 2nd - The wind from the north-northwest with a terrible storm. We could not cook. Rain and hail alternated and it was very cold. I am not ashamed to say that I prayed almost the entire day and wept. I am too weak to describe my misery during this time.

The 3rd - Thank God! The storm has abated. The wind blew hard from the northwest to west. We call it good weather but can not cross the cabin without the risk of breaking our neck or leg. Also, we now have no other ships with us. We are alone. Lord have mercy upon us!

The 4th - A warm southwest wind, very strong. This evening there was frequent thunder and lightning, and again toward morning.

The 5th - A strong southwest wind. The ship shook violently. We have sailed very rapidly on our entire voyage to this point but still we have covered less than one-third of our journey, by my reckoning. God deliver us to England soon! Had I known all of this misery previously, who knows but what I could have been resolute enough to have taken my own life.

The 6th - Southwest wind and a restless sea. We made little headway.

The 7th - Southeast wind, a very calm sea, and the motion of the ship was bearable. Toward twelve o'clock the wind increased but the beautiful weather continued. According to what I hear, we have sailed too far to the south. Toward evening it became stormy and we had a bad night.

The 8th - A strong wind from the south and much rain.

The 9th - Wind from the southwest and still raining. The ship's captain believed we were about as far as the Azores, but 300 miles to the north. If this is true, with God's help we will soon reach England.

The 10th - Westerly but almost no wind. The sea was surprisingly restless, otherwise it was very warm. At three o'clock in the afternoon the wind came from the east, completely contrary.

The 11th - A strong southwest wind, and we sailed ten miles per hour. This was accomplished by rainy weather and it was very cold.

The 12th - The west wind blew hard and it rained heavily. We could not cook, and more thunder than we have had previously. So quickly can the weather change, and it is very cool.

The 13th - A strong southwest wind with much rain. It was nearly impossible to cook. The wind changed at three o'clock this afternoon and came from the northwest so that I hope to see the coast of England tomorrow. This wind is very good for us but I fear a storm. Please God make me wrong.

The 14th - Southwest by south wind. It continued very strong with a terrible and continuous rain. Suddenly at two o'clock in the afternoon a strong breeze arose from the south. The sea became rough and the spray flew. At once high waves built up so that it was difficult to see forty yards. This morning we saw a ship behind us. We believed it belonged to our fleet. However, we put on all possible sail. This night we had a storm.

The 15th - A west wind blew very hard, which we could almost call a storm. I was again miserable, without sleep and our meals only salted pork- +++ unpleasant society. The ship behind us was no longer in sight.

The 16th - A good west wind, a calm sea, but rain in the morning and cold in the afternoon. Otherwise I continue to hope from day to day to see land. According to the reckoning of our ship's captain, we have no hope of being there in less than eight days.

The 17th - A strong southwest wind and very cold. Toward noon high waves developed.

The 18th - A contrary northeast wind and frightfully cold.

The 19th - A northeast wind as contrary as yesterday. It was rather cold and the wind blew hard.

The 20th - A beautiful Sunday, but it was calm with no wind. I was on deck the whole day. We saw many fish, generally a bad sign. During the afternoon a good breeze arose from the south.

The 21st - A contrary northeast wind blew very hard.

The 22nd - A northeast wind with yesterday's weather. Only due to the greatest need was there anything cooked today.

The 23rd - A terrible northeast storm.

The 24th - Again a strong, contrary southeast wind with high seas. A Frenchman died and many people are sick. We were all terribly hungry. A soup was cooked for three hours although the waves beat against the ship. By noon it was a bit better. "I can't ashamed to confess that I dropped Tears the whole day, and sent a great many prayers to our Lord, I felt a great deal considering the bad Fate of my Life time my berthday until now: but I deserve a good deale more, God strong the me"[1] +++ This morning a ship was quite near us. We put on all our sails to get away. Good Lord, what a quarrelsome society!

The 25th - A rather good southwest wind. It was possible to go on deck. It was not light until after nine o'clock. We are apparently close to the coast of Ireland to our north. At noon the wind was bad and it rained.

The 26th - A bad and strong southeast wind. Nothing could be cooked.

The 27th - A storm and rain. In short, the same fate as yesterday.

The 28th - Calm but with a heavy rain. Nevertheless, I went on deck in order to get some fresh air.

The 29th - Calm, beautiful weather. At noon it rained and this continued until evening.

The 30th - A strong, contrary east wind. We saw a ship to the north.

The 31st - An east wind, high seas, and rain like yesterday. Unfortunately, the wind grew very strong and I can not help but complain to Heaven.

The 1st of February - An east wind, rain, a storm with hail, and to tell the truth, it lay a foot deep on the deck. We could not cook, "but what a bad compagne".[2]

The 2nd - The wind still from the east but worse and contrary, rain, cold, a restless sea. We saw two small ships which caused an alarm.

The 3rd - A south wind on this happy day. A gentle and calm sea. We could still see both ships which sailed the same course as we did and apparently were English, also. After we had sent something to eat to the captain today, God be praised, I ate my fill. It rained continuously and was very cold.

The 4th - A gentle south wind, rain, and very cold. This morning we saw a ship behind us. It raised all its sails and in less than two hours had disappeared. We assumed it to have been an enemy. Our ship's captain was ready to defend his ship, which suited us, as we were unarmed invalids.

The 5th - A favorable southwest wind but rain, as on every day.

The 6th - The best possible southwest wind, cold and rainy. The color of the sea changed today and appeared green rather than blue. This gives hope of seeing land. A sloop approached us again this morning and after coming very close, turned away. We were in a serious dilemma. Toward one o'clock the lead was cast and we found bottom at eighty fathoms.

The 7th - The very best of winds from the northwest, cold but without rain. At two o'clock we cast the lead and had bottom at fifty fathoms. We saw a great many ships but none chased after us. Toward evening we had a calm, to our great disappointment.

The 8th - A south wind which was not as good as yesterday. A dull, rainy day. At ten o'clock the lead was cast. We found bottom at 35 fathoms. A sailor sighted land from the mast. During the afternoon the wind became unfavorable and we had to tack, to our disgust. In the evening the wind improved.

The 9th - Calm with an astonishing fog. Toward ten o'clock a little wind arose from the south. The lead was cast and we had bottom at 22 fathoms. We could not be sure, since the sun was not shining, where we were, but the captain was of the opinion, according to the depth, that we were near the Isle of Wight. God be praised for helping us this far! He will continue to watch over us.

The 10th - Calm with weather like yesterday. A terrible fog. We have not advanced since yesterday.

The 11th - A contrary northeast wind. Thank Heaven, for the first time we saw the English coast. What a pleasure! It can not be expressed. We are thirteen Stanges opposite Portsmouth.[3] Because the wind is unfavorable we lost ground. At three-thirty we anchored in the harbor, close to the Isle of Wight. Toward evening a boat came from the warship and took off all our sailors.

The 12th - Very cold with a strong wind. Four ships of our fleet entered. From them we heard that they saw seven ships of our fleet sink during the storm, and our frigate *Solebay* lost three masts and had to return to New York. Heaven only knows how many lives were lost, but God has brought us safely here. Pressing sailors continues very diligently and therefore all of them run away and hide.

The 13th - I went to Portsmouth today and looked over the city, which while small is also quite pleasant. The harbor is especially good and large and the commerce is very noteworthy The defenses are in very good condition. I also noted a great difference in the life style compared to the Americans; those here being very polite to me. At the present time people misjudge the English.

The 15th - Today Lieutenant Strahlendorf went to London and from there to Germany. Admiral [George] Rodney captured a Spanish warship of 64 cannons, five frigates, and 24 transports near Gibralter and the Spanish admiral's ship was sunk.

The 16th - Very cold weather. The ship, which at the start of our voyage from Sandy Hook had been reported as taking water, also sank. The sailors, after three days on the sea in a boat, reached a Dutch ship and have now arrived here.

The 22nd - After the captain has again obtained a crew and we are ready to sail, the wind again is contrary. It is very strong from the north and for the first time since we left New York, we must once again put up with the extreme cold. The salted provisions which I have eaten, unfortunately begin to show their effects. My scurvy swelling causes me much discomfort and at the same time, the number of our sick increases daily. Lord let us soon be put ashore, otherwise much misery will result. At twelve o'clock we were beyond Spithead. Our fleet is more than fifty sail. I can not yet determine our escort. I recognize the frigate *Daphne* and it is my belief that still others must be with such a fleet.

The 23rd - A north wind like yesterday and not very favorable. At twelve o'clock we passed Dover and then tacked back and forth. We anchored near the city at five o'clock. At midnight we entered The Downs and at four o'clock anchored near Deal.

The 24th - A good south wind. We set sail at nine o'clock and passed Margate, a small city. At four o'clock, because of the ebb tide, we anchored. At eleven o'clock at night we again sailed with the flood tide.

The 25th - We anchored at four o'clock in the morning not far from Sheerness, a harbor in the Thames, and at twelve o'clock we began tacking However, because the wind was contrary from the west and a storm wind, which broke something on our middle mast, we had to anchor at two-thirty. At four o'clock the wind raged so terribly that one of the many single-masted sloops cruising near us sank. Although it was not far from us we could not provide any help because our boat was securely fastened on the deck. The crew of the ship all drowned. This misfortune disturbed me greatly. No event has had such an effect on me as this. Many say death is inevitable, but I think this is more gruesome and can not be compared with any other.

The 26th - The north wind was still as strong as yesterday. It is extremely cold and because the storm persisted, we had to remain lying here until midnight.

The 27th - We tacked until we anchored at six o'clock in the morning. The wind was contrary from the west but we tacked from one o'clock until seven, when we anchored near Gravesend. It was a cold, rainy day.

The 28th - Our pilot left us and we could not get another one here. We began tacking again at two o'clock. Because the wind was very contrary we anchored again at three o'clock, near a powder magazine.

The 29th - At four o'clock we again sailed a short distance with the flood tide and an unfavorable wind, until we anchored at eight o'clock. Although our journey is already very boring and unpleasant, the view of both shores is very pleasant. It is worth seeing for everyone. I wish nothing more here than that my health were better, but the scurvy gives me much discomfort.

The 1st of March - At five o'clock in the morning we sailed again with the flood tide and a contrary wind, as far as Woolwich, where we anchored at ten o'clock. The wife of an invalid died. She could not be lowered into the water and therefore, of necessity, I was sent to Woolwich to obtain permission to bury her. It was approved and she was buried at five o'clock on the best place.

The 2nd - We sailed at seven o'clock in the morning, and at ten o'clock finally arrived, after a short voyage, in Deptford, which is 24 miles from London. At noon I traveled in a small boat to the city and upon my arrival heard that our Prince was there. I immediately went to pay my respects and I can say nothing else but that he received me graciously. I also had the great honor of dining with him during the evening.

The 3rd - I completed my business, in so far as possible, with our agent, as this was of some importance and was of great concern to me.

During the evening I again had the great honor of dining with the Margrave.

The 4th - I received money for our remaining journey. My accounts, which were not completed, greatly embarrassed me. I received the order today to deliver them and therefore I was unable to take in the sights of London. I took leave of the Prince this evening, also. The running about has caused a great deal of pain in my scorbutic foot.

The 5th - At ten o'clock I traveled back to Deptford in the common coach and as I was about to change to another carriage at twelve o'clock, to my great displeasure, our baggage was held up by customs. Therefore we had to wait until it could all be inspected. Taxes had to be paid on everything because I insisted on remaining there until I could take everything with us.

The 6th - At noon our baggage was inspected. At three o'clock we boarded a single-masted sloop. At three-thirty we sailed and at six o'clock were again back in Gravesend, where we anchored. That evening I went into the city because there was very little room on our ship.

The 7th - At six o'clock in the morning those troops who could march were disembarked and at seven o'clock we began our march on land to Chatham. I rode in a post chaise and arrived there with the troops at ten o'clock. We were quartered in the barracks. At one o'clock the remaining men and the baggage arrived with the sloop. I had already encountered a part of the Hessian invalids here. Every place is full of English recruits intended for America.

The 8th - A very beautiful day. I took a walk and the region was very pleasing. Also, various fortifications were in the area.

The 13th - An unpleasant time, one day after the other, spent there. Everything of note here, which can be seen in a short time, I have seen. No socializing and no conversation. Why shouldn't I wish soon and preferably to be in Germany in my fatherland?

The 27th - Idleness is the root of all evil. A person goes walking to drive away boredom, then he enters the Post [Inn] and gets drunk, sometimes remaining all night. Sometimes he goes to the Jew, "because he has a fine maid servant, and not of A Natur"[4] +++ In this manner a person goes through the city and acts like a fool, passing himself off as a Frenchman, a Spaniard, or a Russian.

The 6th of April - Since the start of this month we have had unpleasant weather; rain, snow, and cold constantly changing. I strongly wish to leave here because it is an expensive and monotonous place to stay.

The 9th - The weather is still terribly cold and it snows about noontime every day. Today we received the pleasant order that in a few days we are to embark. As I attended a comedy a few days ago, it is necessary for me to mention that, among others, an English officer spoke rather loudly and at once a laborer told him to be quiet. A beautiful lady sat beside me. "I must confess that I fell in love with her. However, she paid me no heed and I found my feelings were in vain."[5] The ribbons of her coiffure nearly blinded me and the next day I could hardly see.

The 13th[6] - After the Hessians were embarked on the twelfth, not only did the time pass very slowly, but I was also embarrassed feeling I might be forgotten. However, when we were embarked in a boat at nine o'clock this morning at Chatham Dockyard, I was lifted over with care. At eleven o'clock we were not far from Sheerness and went at once on board the transport brig *Emerald*. It was a newly-built ship and this was its maiden voyage.

The 16th - We awaited the order to sail. The wind was northwesterly and terribly strong. The water was rather restless.

The 20th - A northwest wind with beautiful weather. We still have no order to sail. The time passes very slowly for me. After I had the ship's captain to dinner today I must record that he drank water with his meal, which is above all, not the usual thing for the English, as in this regard, they are like all nations. They believe that first of all, their customs are in every respect the best in the world, and especially those which, while not seen, would be considered laughable by foreigners.

The 22nd - West-southwest wind. We sailed out of the harbor at two o'clock in the afternoon and anchored where the Thames and Chatham Downs meet. Our escort, the frigate *Levine*, of 32 cannons, also lay there, awaiting the departure on our journey.

The 25th - West wind. At five o'clock this morning the anchor was raised and we set sail. Beautiful weather but very little wind. Our fleet consisted of six ships and our escort frigate *Levine*. We could see the English coast all day and passed Harwich. During the night it rained very hard and the sea was very rough.

The 26th - A north-northwest wind blew very strongly. The seas rose very high and our brig sailed very badly. A very large fleet of coastal vessels approached. I spent the day in bed. At five o'clock a calm set in. The Dutch coast could be seen. At seven o'clock we were in the channel but could not enter and so turned out to sea.

The 27th - A southwest wind and rainy weather. We did not trust ourselves to enter without a pilot as we feared a strong wind gust might cause us to crash or to be thrown on the shore. A pilot came at eleven o'clock and we anchored at twelve o'clock. At two o'clock we entered the Soue River. When we reached Hellevoetsluis we needed another pilot. Therefore, the fleet tacked. There was a terribly stormy wind. Some ships hit against one another and were badly damaged. We ran aground but worked loose after three o'clock and then dropped anchor.

The 28th - At seven o'clock in the morning we set sail and now and then dropped anchor. Although the wind was not favorable for us, among other places, we passed Willemstad, and then anchored at eight o'clock.

The 29th - A very favorable southwest wind with good weather. At eight o'clock in the morning we sailed and at twelve o'clock, God be praised, we arrived at Dordrecht. Lord grant that this is the end of our sea voyage. I am sick of it. At four o'clock in the afternoon the recruits arrived from Nijmegen. Captain Cramon, who commanded them, took charge of my transport.[7]

The 30th - At nine o'clock in the morning we embarked in a Dutch sloop but remained at anchor near the city during the day. It was a rainy day. The city looked pleasant to me because of its cleanliness. Nevertheless, I would not be caught dead in Holland.

The 1st of May - Very beautiful and warm weather. We sailed at five o'clock in the morning but there was almost no wind. We had to halt during the afternoon after having traveled about ten miles.

The 2nd - We sailed at noon, passing Gorinchem, Loewenstein, and Zaltbommel, and anchored about five miles from the latter, at eight o'clock.

The 3rd - After the wind turned against us, we had to remain at anchor.

The 4th - We sailed toward evening and traveled throughout the night.

The 5th - At four o'clock in the afternoon we arrived at Nijmegen. We at once transferred to German boats in which I was not especially pleased.

The 6th - During the afternoon the order was sent to me, in the presence of Captain Cramon, by the commandant that I should continue our trip as soon as possible.

The 7th - We remained lying there, because first we had to send for horses which were to pull our ship.

The 8th - At four o'clock in the afternoon we moved out. We went a short distance. I was happy to get away from the impertinent Dutch.

The 9th - Not far from Cleve, which is Prussian, we visited the last Dutch customs station. We then entered the Rhine and sailed as far as Emmerich, which is Prussian, where we remained overnight.

The 10th - We went a short distance of about seven and one-half miles.

The 11th - We passed Wesel and went about two and one-half miles farther.

The 12th - We sailed as far as Ruhrort,[8] the last Prussian city.

The 13th - At nine o'clock in the evening we passed Duesseldorf, a Pfalz fortification, and Koenigswerde. It was very beautiful weather.

The 14th - A rainy day. First thing today I had to announce our arrival to the governor. Therefore we were delayed until nine o'clock. We halted this evening near Zons.

The 15th - A rainy day. We arrived at Cologne, an imperial city.

The 16th - Because we changed horses here, we had to remain until afternoon. Therefore I had time to do some sightseeing in the city, which was not worth the effort. The Dome, however, from a religious, decorative, and size point of view, is noteworthy. This afternoon we sailed a little farther.

The 17th - At noon we arrived at Bonn and then I had to announce our arrival, as usual, to the governor. However, he was attending mass and so I was taken there. At one o'clock we continued our journey and ten miles beyond (land miles) we anchored.

The 18th - We passed Neuwied, our county, and arrived at Coblenz at seven o'clock. Opposite is Fort Ehrenbreitstein. This city pleased me the most of all those which I saw on our journey. Sergeant [Johann Heinrich] Wiederhold, who had remained behind yesterday, has apparently deserted.

The 19th - At five o'clock in the afternoon we arrived at St. Goar, or the first Hessian fort, Rhinefels. It appeared that our arrival did not especially please the governor. However, we remained overnight.

The 20th - Beautiful weather. We passed Bingen. The mountains came to an end. We remained overnight at Winkel, a small Mainz village.

The 21st - At five o'clock in the afternoon we arrived at Mainz and remained there at anchor overnight.

The 22nd - We departed in the morning, entered the Main River, and at seven o'clock arrived at Frankfurt. The crowd of people was terrible, and we were seen as some kind of monsters.

The 23rd - We left at twelve o'clock and arrived at Hanau at six o'clock.

The 24th - We had a day of rest. I visited the Fasanerie and Wilhelm's Bath, which the Hereditary Prince had laid out.

The 25th - At seven o'clock in the morning we resumed our journey and spent the night two and one-half miles below Aschaffenburg.

The 26th - Very warm weather. During the evening we passed Heubach Loewenstein.

The 27th - We arrived at Wertheim in the evening. The people there whom I had met on the previous march [to America] extended many courtesies to me.

The 28th - We reached Zimmern, opposite Rothenfels, which belongs to Wuerzburg.

The 29th - To Wernfeld, also a village belonging to Wuerzburg.

The 30th - During the evening we arrived at Wuerzburg. It was extremely hot weather.

The 1st of June - At five o'clock in the morning we marched out and at nine o'clock arrived at our quarters in Oberrittelsheim.

The 2nd - We moved out at five o'clock and arrived at Uffenheim at eight o'clock.

The 3rd - We marched again at five o'clock and arrived at Marktbergel, where our quarters were, at nine o'clock.

\- - - - - - -

Note - The contents of this copy of the diary and the original are confirmed. According to an additional comment by a distant relative of the author of the diary - the former von Feilitzsch head forester Weiss, then in that position in the County of Reham - a second part existed, but this can not be found now among the papers left by the von Feilitzsch zu Weinslitz. They will make it available later, if found.

The contents of this copy of the diary are similar to the original.

Edward von Reitzenstein

Lieutenant
Christian Friedrich Bartholomai

Extracts
from the diary
covering the expedition to the southern part of North America

(December 1779 - June 1780)

Translated from a manuscript
in the
New York Public Library

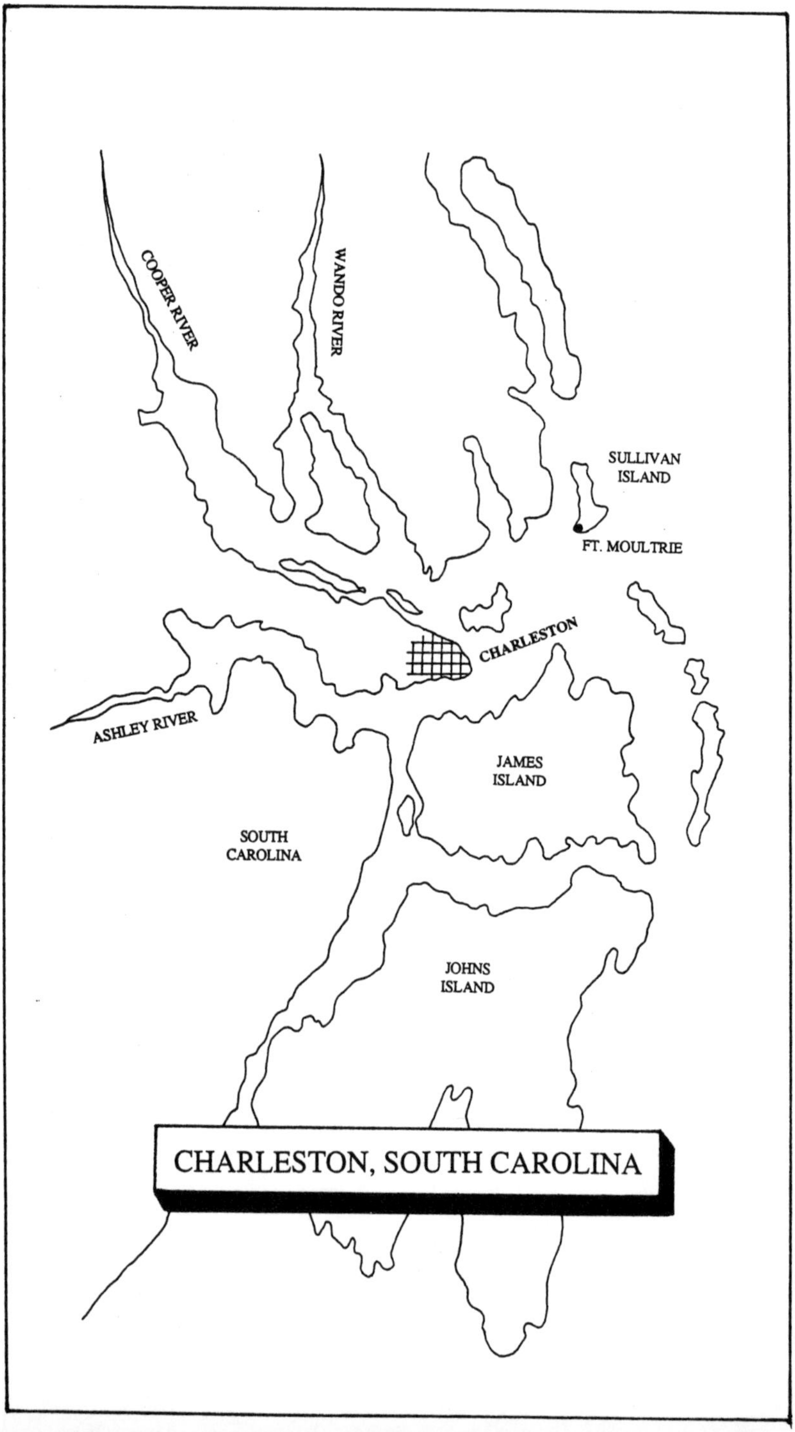
COOPER RIVER
WANDO RIVER
SULLIVAN ISLAND
FT. MOULTRIE
CHARLESTON
ASHLEY RIVER
JAMES ISLAND
SOUTH CAROLINA
JOHNS ISLAND
CHARLESTON, SOUTH CAROLINA

The Bartholomai Diary
Extracts

From the diary of the expedition undertaken by the commander-in-chief in America, Sir Henry Clinton, at the end of the year 1779, to the southern part of North America, and a brief commentary on the American War.

by

C.F. von Bartholomai

Lieutenant of the Ansbach Jaeger Corps

- - - - - - -

As it is my intention to make an extract from the small diary which I kept during the expedition which I accompanied from New York to the southern part of North America during the month of December 1779, it appears necessary for me, as these pages are meant for Europe and so that the reader can grasp the significance of the present war in this distant part of the world, to clarify the situation here, at least during the present war, exactly and correctly, which without exaggeration must be considered one of the most dangerous and important. This is not easy.

A European, even if he judges the present war carefully, will, without having been informed about the existing conditions of our situation, form an adverse opinion of our general commanding in America when I tell him that from a very weak army in New York, a considerable part, and almost the entire elite forces therefrom, was embarked in the dead of winter to make a journey aboard ship, during the most dangerous time, and under the most uncomfortable conditions, in order to capture a fortress at a distance of 800 English miles. Therefore, this project entailed a terrible risk, first because the necessary troops, of those few remaining here, and the accompanying warships, considering the apparent dangers, might be lost, and second, if the fleet were forced to return because of storms or the need for repairs, the reentering of the harbor and the debarkation might be impossible, because at this time of the year, near Sandy Hook, the harbor is completely frozen over or covered with a thick sheet of ice through which it is impossible to penetrate.

In addition, it might be considered that if these troops and warships were lost, England would have suffered an irreplaceable loss, in part because much time and effort are needed to bring 6,000 or

7,000 men here, and in part because the rebels and French would be stronger than the English in America for some time, and during that time could use this advantage against New York or for some other important undertaking.

Considering all these circumstances, a European would be forced to question if the conquest of the fortress were really necessary, why not march over land, which would spare the fleet and, in case the attempt failed, the army could be withdrawn, or better yet, why could the expedition not be postponed until a more favorable time of the year?

To give a meaningful answer to these questions, I will attempt, according to my limited knowledge, to explain the peculiarities of the American War and to point out the differences between it and the European ones, so that the expedition can be judged accordingly.

Therefore, it is my belief that the following three propositions are applicable:

I. The war in America must be conducted primarily from the sea because for the most part the operations of the army are dependent upon the activity of the fleet.

II. The army can accomplish nothing of importance without the support of the fleet, and may,

III. above all, not venture very far inland without risking a great danger.

As we know, America is a large and extensive part of the world and, in order to successfully conduct the war there, it is necessary to have 200,000 to 300,000 men. However, neither the great size of the rebel army, nor the special bravery of the Americans, whom we have learned to respect, would be able to stand in the way of an army of 16,000 to 20,000 English and Germans, if they decided to march through all of America, except for the reason that the land is such a great expanse. But England can not send such a large army here.

If, however, it is assumed that this march could take place, the coast is so long and harbors for small craft so plentiful, that it would be impossible, despite all precautions, to close all the entrances which the inhabitants use for smuggling and obtaining war materials from the French and Spanish. Because of this, an enemy sea power can not be prevented from landing somewhere and thus placing our army between two forces.

From these circumstances it is easy to understand that it is necessary, first of all, that England must control the local waters before the war can be conducted on land, and if the English fleet suffers a reverse, the army can accomplish nothing, which proves my first proposition.

If this point, the supremacy of the English fleet on the water, is accomplished, two important advantages accrue to the army. First, under its protection the recruits and, more importantly, the provisions for the entire army can be brought here safely from Europe. Secondly, it protects the coast from an enemy landing and thus covers the rear of the army. Then the operations on land can begin, but always under the fleet's protection, because, as I said at the start, the land is extensive and the commanding general is forced to act first in the northern and then in the southern provinces. Therefore it is not only necessary for the fleet to serve by escorting the troops swiftly from one place to another, and to cover the troop landings with gun fire, but to carry weapons, munitions, and provisions, because the troops are widely dispersed and separated by great rivers in the trackless areas, and where the storage of forage exists, the army is prevented from attacking under advantageous conditions. This supports my second proposition.

What I said in my third proposition, that the army dare not move far inland without the greatest danger, results in part from the previously noted consideration of the great risk and because of the shortage of forage. All the oats must be brought here from England and the campaign can never begin, because of the shortage of hay, until the grass is high enough to be used as fodder. On the other hand, however, because of the necessity in which we find ourselves, provisions for the army must follow, because enough for subsistence can not be found deep in the countryside.

This circumstance must be more fully explained.

There are very few cities or villages in America, and these lie widely separated. The residences of the inhabitants on their estates are so scattered that it is impossible, in a radius of twenty or thirty miles, because each estate cultivates only a small area, to obtain subsistence even for a corps of several thousand men.

However, these few inhabitants have enough produce to support a corps. Therefore at the first reports of the army's approach, on orders of Congress, all supplies are sent away so that we must always live on our own provisions, transported by the army.

Even though I concede that enough provisions are available and that it would be possible therefore for magazines to be established, which could support the army, as is customary in Europe, it is not possible in America.

For example, I will assume the enemy were defeated in New York province and we must follow it to Pennsylvania. Therefore the army must move 100 miles from its magazines. First, just to occupy the conquered countryside and the magazines which would be set up, a large occupying force would be necessary. Next, more troops would be necessary to escort provisions deep into the land than would be required for the expedition itself. The reason is this - the inhabitants of the land, all of whom are rebels in their hearts and constitute the local militia, can not be trusted for this reason. At the moment all hide themselves under the mask of being king's people, but as soon as our army withdraws the least distance, they secretly assemble and attack our army in the rear and on the flanks. However, the primary concern is that they make the transportation of provisions unsafe and dangerous and there can never be certainty that such provisions will arrive. The rugged terrain is partially responsible for this. However, when the provisions are actually delivered by a large escort, we still lose much throughout the year due to the many skirmishes with the militia and the weakened army, which each year receives only a few recruits. This can not be tolerated. As a result of these circumstances, and examples, I hope to have made clear that the conduct of the American War is unusual and that there is a difference between this and European wars.

How many opportunities a commanding general-in-chief must consider here before he can undertake something, and how many advantageous projects must be allowed to pass because he can not undertake them without the fleet, without mentioning the disappointing delays which must be considered for an expedition because of having to cross a body of water due to storms, tides, and other inconveniences. All these circumstances are unknown to a European commander and despite all these various hindrances, a general in America is compelled to conduct the undertakings, which, from reports of the present war, must seem completely illogical, and which our expedition will be an example.

To these large and apparent differences of the war, I must also note two necessary elements are unavailable to the local general in conducting the war, namely spies and local guides. I am not saying that these two things can not be had, but rather that they are insufficient. Concerning the spies, it is difficult here because such a man, in a country where everyone is the enemy, can learn little of what is desired and at times, nothing at all. On the other hand, nothing can be attempted nor can the parties trust one another.

Concerning the local guides, they are very much, almost entirely, controlled by the general-in-chief and as the war must be conducted in so many various regions, the commanding general often has no available guides. How can they provide help then for a staff officer who must conduct a small expedition? And when help is provided by a guide, the cost of providing the same for a junior officer is too expensive, as they cost fourteen or more Spanish dollars. Efforts have been made by the use of special signs to offset this shortage, but in part they have been inadequate, in part they do not indicate all the short cuts, and can not always be trusted, as I myself have learned.

Opposed thereto is the enemy general who is well supplied with these two items. First, every inhabitant is his spy, and second, he or his troops are absolutely familiar with the land and he is given timely notice of every moment by his enemy, which is provided by the many listeners. Yes, the most unpleasant and most dangerous factor for the local general consists of the situation that because we need vegetables and other foodstuffs, we are compelled to allow every spy, dressed as a farmer, free entry and exit from our camps, and they know well how to take advantage of this situation.

When such a farmer learns something about us, he immediately mounts a horse, which year in and year out he has had grazing in a fenced off piece of land not far from his house. He hastens over hill and dale by a back road to another estate. The neighbor, in the same manner, takes the report to a third person, and so forth until it is delivered to headquarters.

Even the ordinary soldier must be able to understand the difference between a European war and one in America because he must frequently go aboard ship, tolerate a sea voyage, going in a short time from a cold climate to a warm one or from a warm climate to a cold one.

In short, just the thought that an army of 16,000 to 20,000 men would detach a corps of 6,000 to 7,000 men and send it 800 miles away, would rightly be considered a great folly, which in America, however, is a reality and often employed.

Now I come to our expedition.

At the beginning I will make a suggestion as to why the expedition was not preferably made on land, or at least postponed, since I have already pointed out that the army never dared to penetrate deeply inland, and with such a small corps, to undertake an 800 mile march in the dead of winter, through provinces occupied only by enemies, across great rivers, would be the height of insanity.

Still, I am not able to clearly explain that the expedition was absolutely necessary and under no circumstances could it have been postponed.

Therefore it is necessary to understand the situation in which our army found itself.

At the start of the year 1779, the English, except for Canada and a small island, controlled only the city of New York and a district of about twenty miles in circumference, Long Island, Staten Island, Rhode Island, Paulus Hook, and Halifax in all of America, and only at the end of the year 1778 had General [Augustine] Prevost been able to capture the city of Savannah in Georgia.

Our army in New York, due to the reinforcements sent to Savannah, Halifax, Pensacola, and St. Augustine, was seriously weakened and the local fleet was barely able to maintain its stations. Opposing us the rebels had a good standing army and a large French fleet to support it. Although the general-in-chief could not undertake the least decisive action, he cleverly decided, in part to prevent [George] Washington from attacking our position and in part to cut the communications with White Plains, to send some troops up the North River to capture the two forts at Stony and Verplanck's Points, and to give the enemy something to do in his own country. General [William] Tryon with several thousand men was sent up the East River and made several attacks along the coast. In addition to these operations, [Charles, Earl] Cornwallis, with all the men who could be spared here, was ordered to Savannah to reinforce General Prevost, but due to the most unfortunate luck, had to turn back without accomplishing his objective due to contrary winds.

We were in this situation when the French fleet appeared, whose operations on land and water could not be given the least impediment by our few ships.

Now it was necessary for all of us to expect additional expeditions and to look to our own defense and safety.

Therefore we abandoned the two conquered forts on the North River and, to secure the land side of York Island, a great defensive line was laid out above Fort Knyphausen. The smaller outlying works from Fort Independence to Number 8 were demolished. And, as experience had taught that Rhode Island could not be held without the protection of a good fleet, and that there was a serious risk that the defenders, who were Ansbachers for the most part, would be captured, this island was completely abandoned.

These precautionary measures were also necessary because the French, by their return, had demonstrated their intention to undertake this easily accomplished conquest.

Meanwhile the enemy plan was as follows: The French were to capture the only English occupied place in the southern part of North America, that is, Savannah, which was weakly garrisoned, and make themselves masters of Georgia. If this were successfully carried out, General Washington was to attack New York from two sides, from the land side at Kingsbridge and across Staten Island, for which purpose a corps had been assembled near Fort Lee in New Jersey.

In order to carry out this well-formed plan, [Charles Hector] Comte d'Estaing landed several thousand French troops near Savannah during the fall and joined a rebel corps under General [Benjamin] Lincoln. Fortunately, Comte d'Estaing conducted a long correspondence with the old General Prevost, giving him time to assemble his widely scattered troops and giving the engineer [James] Moncrief, with the help of several hundred driven-together Negroes, time to throw up some defenses, hurriedly, to protect the city. When Comte d'Estaing was convinced of General Prevost's intentions, his anger caused him to launch an all-out attack which resulted in his receiving a serious wound and many other losses, including the respected [Casimir] Pulaski, who had his own corps, to be beaten back. It was necessary for d'Estaing to return to his ships and the rebels quickly departed on land.

This singularly fortunate incident suddenly changed the entire situation in America and gave the English time and opportunity to recover. As Comte d'Estaing had called upon Savannah to surrender in the name of the French king, it was also the French intention to take the city by storm. The importance of occupying the same, which had been realized too late, and which, because of its weak defenses made it now appear open for conquest, was this.

As Congress, or more correctly, all the rebel provinces are short of money with which to buy materials of war such as weapons, munitions, uniforms, and above all medicines, from the French and Spanish, these items are paid for with the products of the land. Indigo, rice, cotton, tobacco, wood for ship building, turpentine, and all these items are products of the southern provinces which are shipped out through the harbors at Savannah and Georgia.

So now, not just to prevent another French attack, and not just to protect Savannah from an attack by the rebels, it was necessary to send a reinforcement and to become master of Charleston, because this harbor controlled South Carolina just as Savannah controlled Georgia.

However, after fully considering that the French would not lightly yield their presence there and knowing that in the coming spring another French fleet was to be expected, and that above all, an army could not tolerate camping in the field, undertaking siege operations, nor conducting long marches there during the heat, beginning in June, it was necessary to begin the expedition immediately and to have concluded it by the end of May.

In this situation the commanding general-in-chief, Sir Henry Clinton, who had been granted unlimited authority by Parliament to conduct the war as he thought best, knowing he would create enemies regardless of his actions, had no other option than to make a choice between two evils. He had to leave the English grasp in Georgia as it was and forget trying to enlarge it, which gave the enemy control of the treasury, or he must decide to undertake an expedition before the end of the year, despite the dangers involved, because of the greater advantage which could result for England. Therefore, he chose to undertake this important measure. I believe, after outlining all the opposing arguments in another place concerning the threatening misfortunes, that the expedition to Charleston in the winter was necessary and could not have been conducted in a better manner.

- - - - - - -

With this in mind, completing the work on the line near Kingsbridge was pushed twice as hard, the warships lying here were made ready, and many transports were loaded with provisions. At the beginning of December Vice Admiral [Marriot] Arbuthnot sent several frigates out to determine if the ships returning to France from Comte d'Estaing's fleet had actually departed.

These preparations could not be carried out in such a secretive manner that Washington would not learn about them.

Therefore, he not only sent an order alerting General Lincoln, the commander in the southern part of North America, but also detached some troops from his army to go there, which, however, on the long march in the middle of the cold weather, resulted in most of the men deserting.

Also the troops in New England, as well as those in New Jersey, made various movements, but the commanding general did not react to them, but only drew the regiments and corps assigned to the expedition gradually closer together.

December 1779

The 15th - The frigate *Roebuck*, which had been sent out, returned and brought the news that Comte d'Estaing had returned to Europe with a part of his fleet and the ocean was now safe. Thereupon the transport ships received orders to obtain fresh water and then to anchor close to York Island.

At the same time the ships returning to England for repairs were to be prepared to sail and to take on board the invalids and those being recalled from the English and German regiments.[1]

Because the army would be seriously weakened by these departures, the inhabitants of New York City volunteered to help with the duty in the city in an emergency.

As a result, additional regiments and corps designated to accompany this expedition marched out of their assigned winter quarters and moved close to New York in order to be embarked.

From the English: The 7th, 23rd, 33rd, 63rd, 64th, and 71st Regiments; two battalions of light infantry commanded by Lieutenant Colonel [Robert] Abercromby; two battalions of grenadiers commanded by Lieutenant Colonel [John] Yorke; the New York Volunteers commanded by [John] Althouse of the Sharp-shooters Corps; Ferguson's Corps; Lord Cathcart's Legion, both foot and mounted, under the command of Lieutenant Colonel [Banastre] Tarleton.

From the German troops: Four battalions of Hessian grenadiers commanded by Major General [Heinrich Julius] von Kospoth; the Huyn Infantry Regiment; 100 of the so-called chasseurs which were formed with men from the Hessian infantry regiments and were commanded by the Hessian Jaeger Captain [George] Hanger,[2] who is an adjutant for General Clinton; and a detachment of Hessian and Ansbach jaegers. All these troops, according to the best calculations, without engineers, but including the artillerymen commanded by Major [Peter] Traille; 100 pioneers and guides, marines, and sailors, amount to 6,975 men.

General Clinton, Lord Cornwallis, Major Generals [Alexander] Leslie, [Johann Christoph] von Huyn, and von Kospoth, as well as Brigadier General [James] Paterson, also went with the expedition.

The following warships sailed as the escort, under the command of Vice Admiral Arbuthnot, with the blue flag: 1) *Robust*, 74-guns 2)

Russell, 74-guns 3) *Europa*, 64-guns 4) *Raisonnable*, 64-guns 5) *Defiance*, 64-guns 6) *Renown*, 50-guns 7) *Roebuck*, 44-guns, carrying Lord Cornwallis 8) *Romulus*, 44-guns, carrying the commander-in-chief 9) *Defoe*, 32-guns, and 10) *Perseus*, 20-guns.

The challenge was Number 59; the reply, Howe.

Each ship's captain received a sealed envelope in which the place was written noting the fleet's destination. However, this was not to be opened, under the strictest punishment, until the ship had been completely separated from the fleet and had not seen it for several days.

All the officers were ordered to sell their horses and to supply themselves with rations for several weeks.

The 19th - The Jaeger Detachment, consisting of 195 Hessians and 55 Ansbachers, none of whom were recruits, marched out of their huts near Morris' house, above Fort Knyphausen, during a cold spell and marched along a hard-frozen road to New York. Eight officers were with them, namely, from the Hessians: Major [Philipp] von Wurmb, Captains [Johann] Ewald, [Johann] Hinrichs, and [Franz Christian] von Bodungen, and Lieutenants [Johann Ernst] Winzingerode and [Johann] Scheffer; from the Ansbachers: Myself and Lieutenant [Jacob Ernst] Kling. Most went aboard the ship *Apollo*, but Captain Ewald and Lieutenant Winzingerode, with fifty jaegers, went aboard the brig *Pan*.

The ship *Apollo*, on which I sailed, was about five years old, had 44 guns; twelve of which were left behind, however, to make room for the jaegers. As a result, the ship rolled more than usual. The ship's captain, John Adamson, was a stingy and, like most ship's masters, not an especially polite man. Instead of 25 sailors, he had only nineteen on board, including four or five very young lads. The mate was an old man, an incompetent and degenerate fellow, responsible for harmony, discipline, and cleanliness on the ship.

The 20th and 21st - We remained at anchor near the wharf at New York while the remaining troops were embarked. The days were bright but the cold was penetrating. This region, which is called The Narrows, was opposite Long Island and already covered with thick ice. We heard that the general-in-chief had given the command over the troops remaining behind to Lieutenant General [Wilhlem] von Knyphausen.

The 22nd - Together with the many ships which had taken on cargo, we sailed to Sandy Hook, where the New York harbor begins, and lay at anchor near the lighthouse.

The fleet for England with the invalids and returnees on board, consisting of nearly 100 ships, still lay at anchor here.

The 23rd - Today we had to remain at anchor, although the wind was favorable, because the artillery and munitions had not yet arrived aboard ship. The fleet bound for England departed, however.

The 24th - The warships which were to be our escort dropped anchor just outside the harbor.

The 25th - Most of our fleet arrived near us from New York, and the horses for the cavalry were hurriedly loaded on board.

The 26th - All the remaining ships followed early this morning and at twelve-thirty in the afternoon we raised anchor. The weather was bright and the movement of the fleet, consisting of 96 sail, presented a pleasant view. Later the northwest wind was very favorable for us. However, while exiting the harbor, near Sandy Hook, the discipline which was customary during Lord [Richard] Howe's command was not seen.

The 27th - Already today our favorable northwest wind began to fade and toward evening only a weak, dissimilar breeze was stirring. This caused our ship to develop an unpleasant roll and did not bode well for us. At evening a complete calm set in, indicative of an approaching storm. Unfortunately, it struck us early and about midnight a strong, contrary wind arose which in a few minutes became a storm. All the sails had to be lowered, the rudder was tied fast, and the ship was given over to the wind and waves. As the night was quite dark, because there was no moonlight, and because the fleet had to remain close together, we were in great danger of ramming another ship or of sinking from some other cause.

The 28th - All day today and during the night, the storm continued with such fury that the entire fleet was scattered. Anyone who has traveled on the sea already knows the discomfort such a storm causes. He can also imagine all the unpleasantness which six persons closed in a small cabin experience, surrounded by a great amount of baggage, during the continuing storm, when a hundred small items tear loose and fly about. If it is also considered that this storm was in the winter, when we could not have a fire for heat, it will be easy to understand what a cold body and an empty stomach had to put up with, because, as is known, cooking is not allowed during a storm. However, all of this was of little consequence considering the deadly danger lurking in the midst of such a large fleet on a pitch black night with the frequent fearful shouting of the sailors.

The 29th - At noon the storm abated somewhat, and we noted a sad result of the storm. The ship *Anna*, on which there were 100 jaegers of Althouse's Company and, as we later learned, thirty of our jaegers, in the previous night had lost the middle and after masts, when rammed by the large hospital ship. Thereafter it drifted about among the ships of the fleet. As the ship carrying the horses was not to be seen, either, our sailors assumed it had foundered. This storm struck between Cape May and Cape Charles. During the afternoon the wind was tolerable but not favorable for us.

The 30th - During the morning the wind eased from hour to hour, until it became completely calm during the afternoon. The air was as warm as it is in Germany in the summer. We were still fifteen sea miles from North Carolina. As pleasant as we found this change in the weather, so unpleasant was the whirlwind which struck us toward evening, accompanied by sharp flashes of lightning, and once again the ships of the fleet sailed in a confused manner. Our ship was also in no small danger as we were suddenly driven toward the admiral's ship. Fortunately, the admiral's ship made a slight turn and we backed our sails. In this manner we prevented the disaster. About midnight a contrary wind arose again and allowed us to go to sleep.

The 31st - Because of the contrary wind and the persistent cold weather, the last day of the year was very unpleasant for us. We also had a continuous heavy rain which increased our displeasure.

January 1780

The 1st - The day was like yesterday with strong, cold rain, contrary wind, and a sky full of thick clouds, so that everyone was in a melancholy mood.

The 2nd - This day was even stormier and a bad day for us. The wind had changed to a storm yesterday and drove us directly toward the rocky and dangerous coast of Cape Hatteras. The mate had already told the crew that the water was shallower by the hour and there appeared to be no method of escaping disaster. Deathly fear was to be seen in every face and we expected at any moment to founder, but the storm then noticeably changed. The admiral used this situation to signal the ships to turn, and with the help of the current we were able to prevent being driven nearer to the coast.

As I have mentioned the current, I will describe it here. Into the Gulf of Mexico, which is actually an ocean, flow wide, strong, and very large rivers, from Florida, Louisiana, Mexico, and other provinces. These waters, joined together, force themselves, with an unbelievable great force, through a narrow gap which is called the Bermuda Straits. The force is so great that even with the best of winds, it is impossible to sail against it.

This gigantic stream of water, which is called the drift, or the current, runs along the coast of North America, toward the north by east, and is strongest near Cape Hatteras. It then weakens somewhat but continues with strength to Cape Cod, because of the many rivers running into the ocean and is noticeable as far as New York.

Despite these incidents, the storm did not cease but continued throughout the night.

The 3rd - The storm appeared to have grown stronger. The movements which the endangered ship made were so violent that it appeared at any moment the masts would break and the pieces tear loose. In such deathly anxiety, during which the ship repeatedly fired emergency shots, we spent the night, completely exhausted in both body and spirit.

The 4th - The storm eased slightly during the morning although the wind remained strong and contrary, accompanied by rain and sleet, which made it very cold. The sea remained very rough and the waves rose up like the highest mountains. Our sailors assured us that they had never seen a storm of equal strength and duration, which is easy to believe, because from the month of December until February, because of the usual storms, not a single ship, let alone a fleet, risks entering the ocean. However, the war makes half of the impossible, possible. As the water in the ship had risen without being suspected, and had risen to over twelve feet, an inspection was made and the leak discovered. It was under the cabin, above the steering rudder. Therefore in a place where it could be repaired and was fixed as well as conditions allowed. It was also done just in time as nightfall was approaching when the storm again increased and on

The 5th - day and night, and on

The 6th - raged with unbelievable fury. It is not possible to describe the misery and fear which we faced. Furthermore, the provisions, which had been taken along to last three, or at most four weeks, ran out and what little was left had to be used sparingly.

The 7th - The storm abated but still a cold, contrary wind remained all day and night, and only on

The 8th - were the sails raised and the steering rudder untied.

The sailors caught a ravenous fish called a shark. It often feeds on salt meat, which is lowered into the water on a line. When trying to bite the meat, it is caught on a very large fishhook. It was nine feet long and weighed about 100 pounds, had three rows of teeth with which it could easily bite off a man's leg, and its rather dark skin was so hard and rough that it could be used as a very fine file. The upper portion of the jaw is unmovable so that when it wishes to swallow its prey, it must roll over on its back. Although it was a male, when cut open, more than forty live young were found inside the body, because, like the toad, it swallows the young when danger threatens, and can later release them.

As a rule, a small brown fish swims ahead of the shark and for this reason it is called a pilot fish. This fish has spines in the lower part of its tail section, rather sharp and comparable to a curry-comb, with which it firmly holds onto the shark's body when danger is present. It must also be noted that neither the stormy weather nor the strong rolling of the ship has ceased. Its flesh is tough and only a small portion on the end of the body, near the tail, is edible.

The 9th - The wind and weather continued raw and unfavorable, but on

The 10th - grew lighter again. The wind was also gentle and favorable. Because of a shortage of zwieback the sailors came near mutiny against the captain, but this situation was resolved by the other officers.

The 11th - Our pleasure faded along with the good wind today and the former contrary wind arose as before. The wind died down about midnight, only to come up with renewed strength.

The 12th - The storm struck again with heavy rain and sleet and it became frightfully cold.

The 13th - During the afternoon the storm began to slacken and a strong, contrary wind made it necessary for the admiral to sail so that the ships could draw closer together.

The 14th - The wind continued just as strong so that while many ships fired distress shots, none was able to provide assistance.

The 15th - A stormy whirlwind replaced the former wind and caused the fleet a great amount of trouble. Nevertheless, on

The 16th - the sea was quite tolerable. The transport ship *George*, with light infantry on board, took advantage of this opportune time and raised an emergency flag. The fleet halted and, upon a signal from Captain [Thomas] Tonken, each ship in the fleet lowered a small boat into the water to be used to carry the men of the *George* to other ships. Those individuals were so distraught from experiencing the fear of death, that everyone exerted great effort to insure the men and their possessions were taken off in the boats sent to their rescue. They were very apathetic. The removal had barely been completed when the wind again increased. It was necessary to take in all the sails and make all provisions for giving the ship over to the wind and waves.

The 17th - The wind eased a bit. We counted the ships still together and found 39 still present. A warship was ordered to seek out the scattered ships.

The 18th - The wind was more favorable, but the current which had caught us, pushed us backward six miles every hour. This disrupted our voyage once again. All the troops were removed from the transport ship *Swan*, which had developed a serious leak. Toward evening the sky grew brighter, the weather became pleasant, and during the night a calm developed.

The 19th - The wind became contrary again, but not as strong. The crew of the ship *Juno*, which had sprung a leak, transferred to other ships. This too was accomplished just in time as at eleven o'clock midday a signal was given to prepare the sails and masts against another storm.

The 20th - The storm eased but the wind continued strong and unfavorable.

The 21st - The weather was cold with rain and sleet, and very unpleasant for us poor creatures in the cabin, as the wicked wind frequently blew the smoke from the coal fire into the cabin. Captain Ewald passed near us today and informed us that his ship and four others had collided in The Narrows at New York and that his men had been transferred to other ships.

The 25th and 26th - The wind and weather were cold, dull, and gloomy but the admiral strove to maintain his desired course.

The 27th - The sky finally cleared and the wind blew favorably. During the night a storm arose, which this time served to our advantage.

Today I reached a conclusion concerning the extent that being accustomed to something controls us. During the first storm everyone was despondent, during the next, passive, and during the last one, we had become so accustomed that none of us took the least note of the violent movement of the ship nor the high waves. On the other hand, the salt provisions, with all their unpleasantness, were wolfed down without any qualms.

The 28th - Such an unusual cold set in that despite the unbearable smoke, we were compelled to have a fire in the cabin. We cast the lead and found bottom at 25 fathoms. Although this was a more than adequate depth of water, we had to take in most of the sails and proceed with great caution because this entire coast is full of sandbanks.

The 28th and 29th - During the afternoon the sailors discovered land ahead from the top of the mast. While daylight still lasted, we hurried onward. However, as we had only nine fathoms at nine o'clock, we had to tack.

The 30th - The wind was very weak. We learned from a ship's captain, when he approached near us, that he had become separated from the fleet and broken open his sealed orders. The assembly point for the fleet was at Tybee, an island not far from Savannah. At noon Commodore [John] Henry, who was stationed at Savannah, arrived on the frigate *Fowey*, accompanied by a sloop, to see the admiral. We were then given the signal to be prepared to anchor. Meantime the admiral took the warships away in order to reconnoiter the Port Royal River. We continued our journey under the command of Captain Tonken.

The 31st - Today the weather was very mild but so foggy that it was impossible to see the least speck of land. This is the rare fog which hindered [Christopher] Columbus so much upon his discovery of America. It is not like the usual fog on land, but stretches for thirty miles of more over the ocean and so thick that ships traveling very close together can not see one another. Therefore it is necessary to signal their presence to one another by beating drums, shooting, and blowing horns.

Toward noon a calm set in. We still had seven and one-half fathoms of depth. The warships returned, but because of the shallow water, anchored somewhat farther from land. The *Romulus* took over command and at three o'clock gave the signal to anchor. This occurred later at four-thirty in the Georgia roadstead between Tybee Island and the harbor at Port Royal. As the fog would not clear and the ships were still not close together, the admiral gave a signal every half hour from the ocean by means of a cannon shot, which was answered each time by the *Romulus*.

February 1780

The 1st - We again weighed anchor and sailed toward Tybee Island. The wind was very weak and therefore the fog was even thicker. We had to sail with the lead being constantly cast. As our ship's captain did not heed the sailors calling the depth from time to time, before we were aware, we went aground on a sandbank during the evening and the ship settled slightly on its right side.

The 2nd - Before daybreak Captain Tonken sent several boats to transfer us onto land. As it was pitch black and because the ship was wet due to the heavy fog, making the coming and going very dangerous, everyone remained aboard the ship and waited for the flood tide, which, with the help of some more sailors from the fleet, freed us at about four o'clock in the morning. However, as it was still not light enough to get underway, we immediately dropped anchor again. Finally we set sail again at nine o'clock, but as there was almost no wind, we traveled mostly by being towed by sailors in small boats, until we were able to rejoin the other transport ships near the lighthouse in Savannah Sound. Captain Ewald came aboard our ship today and told us about the circumstances of his shipwreck. His fifty jaegers were put aboard two other ships, including thirty on the ship *Anna*, which had encountered misfortune and not returned to us. During the end of May we learned that it had been driven to England.

A perfect example of sea travel! When an individual who wanted to go from New York south to Charleston, which is 800 miles away, travels several thousand miles to the north and arrives in England.

What the troops on this voyage experienced is beyond description, as can be understood from the following.

Of the 46 days spent aboard ship from New York here, we traveled 36, including 25 days and nights of storms and thirteen days with contrary winds. Four or five ships had to be unloaded on the high seas and as of this date, ten transports and a warship are still missing. Of the horse ships, not a single one has yet arrived. Add to this the unpleasant and unhealthy coal smoke which every movement of the ship drives into the cabin.

As we had to wait for a time for the missing ships and in part so that the general-in-chief could discuss the pending operations with General Prevost, I took the opportunity, while we lay at anchor, to learn the following about Tybee Island

Tybee Island lies at 31° 54' north latitude. The air was as warm as in May. It has, as does all Georgia, a soil which is white, sandy, and cut up by swamps and small streams, and produces nothing but the famous palmetto cabbage tree and small shrubs, among which is a sort of wild tea, which gives off an aromatic odor. On the right side this island borders on a part of the mouth of the Savannah Sound and on the left is separated from the mainland by a creek. It is possibly twenty miles long and three or four miles wide, and at this time, because the French destroyed the only three houses on the island and drove the residents off, the island is desolate except for the lighthouse.

The abandoned horses and pigs which have grown wild here are consumed with relish by the English. As I have mentioned the palmetto trees, I will give a description of them here.

These trees grow leaves without a stem, from the top. Such a leaf has the identical form of a woman's fan and grows to an astonishing size. I have seen one which was large enough to completely cover a man. At maturity the tree, of twenty or thirty feet and a foot thick, develops in the middle of the top of the trunk, a bud, which, larger or smaller, according to the size of the tree, appears like a sugar cone and consists entirely of fine, white, soft, and almost completely grown-together and immature leaves, which raw and uncooked, taste like cabbage, only somewhat sweeter than the best part. This gives the tree its name. In the middle of the bud is a sweet juice. The most remarkable thing about this tree is first, that it has no branches, and second, its wood is as limber as cork. Therefore it serves incomparably well for ship's masts and for constructing batteries, because the largest cannonballs can not penetrate it. We also find a sort of bird here called a turkey buzzard, of which there are a great many in Georgia and the Carolinas. They somewhat resemble the Indian partridge, having the same size and shape, also the head and neck are bald. In part they resemble the imperial eagle, whose color they have. However, their claws show that they are not birds of prey. They live on snakes, vermin, and carrion, for which reason killing them is punishable by a large fine. Above all, the flesh is not fit to eat because of the strong smell.

The 3rd - Today the ship *Spring*, with recruits for the Savannah garrison regiments of Wissenbach and D'Angelelli, sailed to Savannah. Captain Ewald and Lieutenant Winzingerode, who had gone aboard the vessel after their shipwreck, came aboard our ship. The commander-in-chief sailed to Savannah today, also, and the admiral sailed with the warships, except for the *Vigilante*, which was on station here, and several row galleys, to Port Royal, to take position there.

We heard today that the Spaniards had captured the fort at Mobile in Florida and taken a company of Waldeck grenadiers prisoner.

Three hundred Cherokee Indians have arrived at Savannah, who, because of their barbarity, will not be used on this expedition.

Several of the missing ships rejoined our fleet today.

As our boats sailed to Savannah, Captain Hinrichs had to make this short trip and later told us the following about Georgia. The land is so sandy and infertile that it is necessary to send twelve or more miles inland to get lettuce or other green vegetables. As there is a great shortage of grass, nature has provided another means of feeding cattle, horses, and sheep. A special kind of moss grows on the trees, whose description, because it has strange peculiarities and I have often used it on this expedition, and have a thorough knowledge about it, I will present here. This moss consists of long threads as thick as a weak string and every half inch a finger length growth which intertwines so that in time a cluster about as thick as a man is formed. It is attached on the underside of the branches by a very fine, small root and hangs down from the tree to the ground so that it appears as if the woods is draped with genuine flax. As long as it hangs on the tree, or is kept dry for a few days, it remains green and the usual fodder for the cattle. When it falls on the ground, however, it loses its green skin and takes on the form of horse hair. The inhabitants therefore use it to stuff chairs, mattresses, and saddles.

Above all, Georgia, like the eastern third of South Carolina, is full of snakes of all kinds and other vermin. Also in this province there are many crocodiles, which are called alligators. These make travel so dangerous in the summer that when the residents send a Negro from one plantation to another, they first let him wrap his feet to protect himself against the bite of these poisonous animals. The so-called rattlesnake is the most poisonous. Its bite was considered incurable for a long time. Finally, some years ago, a governor offered a great reward to anyone who could develop an antidote for this strong poison. Then a Negro discovered several roots which could completely counteract this snake's poison. He allowed himself to be bitten by such a snake, did not take these roots until the poison had spread throughout his body, and then in a few days had fully recovered. The reason there are so many vermin in this region, is this: The land has a sandy and saturated with water soil that spreads over several miles as swamp, which is very good for breeding these insects. To this is added the extensive woods, in which there is much water and many morasses, and then the great heat, which incubates the eggs of the vermin, and the scarcity of cold winters, so it is easy to understand why this is the habitat of so many poisonous animals.

The weather today was as pleasant as during the month of May in Germany.

The 4th - Today two more of the missing ships rejoined us.

The 5th - The wind changed today and the weather suddenly turned cold. Several row galleys and armed boats from Savannah joined our fleet.

The 6th - Because of the frequent rain and thick fog, the weather today was very unpleasant. Several missing ships came in. During the afternoon an agent came to our ship and gave the order to our sailors that in case of a landing they were not to engage in plundering for fear of the most severe punishment.

The 7th - Some sleet accompanied the cold weather and we were assured by the oldest people that such an event had never occurred previously. The ship loaded provisions for forty days today. The general-in-chief and the admiral both returned from Savannah today. The *Roebuck* raised the admiral's flag and General Clinton went aboard the agent's ship.

The 8th - The fleet was ordered to be prepared to get underway. Meanwhile a recently arrived transport ship, which had a leak, was unloaded.

Now everyone speculates as to how and where the general-in-chief will attack Charleston. Finally, having learned how the project would be executed, which we initially had to guess, I will now, on 8 February, outline General Clinton's plan, in order to give the reader the opportunity to thoroughly evaluate this venture.

Charleston can be attacked from three sides; from the sea by the army, from the land across the Cooper River from Savannah, and from the islands. But the Cooper River route is not a possibility as we are not masters of North Carolina and the local region, nor from the sea, as the harbor is protected by Sullivan's Island. Therefore, the general-in-chief had to choose the side from the islands. To mask this intention from the enemy, the warships in the Port Royal River made various movements and General Paterson had to march with his corps from Savannah toward Charleston. This project, fortunately, went well. As a consequence, the fleet, consisting of about sixty sail, on

The 9th - weighed anchor at nine o'clock in the morning and entered the North Edisto River. The wind was very weak and we could not sail very far. We anchored at evening near Trench Island.

The 10th - We resumed our voyage, in beautiful, warm weather and with a gentle breeze, among the many beautiful, little islands and anchored at dark near Hunting Island.

The 11th - We saw several enemy ships in the distance which appeared to be observing us. They immediately withdrew. Toward twelve o'clock noon, we were among islands, near the mainland, grouped like a half-moon, which formed a harbor. The admiral, by means of a signal, ordered the flatboats lowered into the water and the ships' captains were to report to Captain Tonken to receive secret orders concerning the debarkation. We immediately dropped anchor.

For our debarkation we received the following orders;

The 1st debarkation - Light Infantry and British Grenadiers

The 2nd debarkation - Hessian Grenadiers, Jaeger Detachment, and 33rd Regiment

The 3rd debarkation - 7th, 23rd, 63rd, 64th English and Hessian Huyn Regiments.

In further orders the army was divided into the following brigades, under Lord Cornwallis:

The Hessian Grenadiers commanded by Major General von Kospoth

The 7th and 23rd Regiments commanded by Lieutenant Colonel [Alured] Clarke

The 33rd and 71st Regiments commanded by Lieutenant Colonel [James] Webster

The 63rd and 64th Regiments commanded by General von Huyn.

The first debarkation began at five o'clock in the evening. The general-in-chief and Lord Cornwallis landed with it. The second debarkation was to begin also, but because of darkness and a heavy rain, it was postponed.

The 12th - At eight o'clock the second division debarked. We were put ashore on Simmons Island which is a point on Johns Island, about six or seven miles from our ship. We took along provisions for three days. We remained here until the remaining troops were landed.

As we were not familiar with this island and had no guide with us, we were misled by a naval officer who had never previously been on this coast, knew very little about the land, and who led us around for several hours through the woods and water in a fog which settled in. Things were no better for the troops who had landed yesterday. Because they had no one to show them the way, they had to spend the night in the woods. What losses this corps could have suffered during a pitch black, very rainy night, in an unfamiliar woods, if this island had been occupied by only a few hundred militiamen.

After a march of eight or nine English miles, we camped just beyond Simmons' house, close to which the headquarters was located, in a woods. The Light Infantry moved as far as Wilson's plantation, eight miles farther ahead. Simmons Island is only six or seven miles long and two or three miles wide, of which hardly a fourth is developed due to almost everywhere being marshy woodland. There is a large rice plantation here because this wet region can produce nothing more. Large sponges lie in the ocean.

The 13th - We marched from ten o'clock in the morning until three o'clock in the afternoon to Wilson's house, which is on Johns Island. The road was nice and level, through solid woods, and like the most splendid avenue. The Light Infantry moved to Chisholm's and Fenwick's plantations on the left bank of the Stono River. As we are still not in control of the river, provisions for the army must be sent along the Bohicket Creek. Here, for the first time, I ate the Carolina sweet potato, which is about a finger long and two fingers thick. They are more like roots than potatoes and taste like carrots, but much sweeter. They are best when they are roasted and hot. Because they are used as a vegetable, they must be peeled and cut up before cooking, otherwise they darken and appear unappetizing. We have seen the Virginia nightingale here, which is one of the most beautiful birds in the world. They are completely vermillian and have an upright tuft on their head shaped like a sugar loaf, and only on the red beak are to be seen some black feathers which give the bird the appearance of having a beard. The size is similar to the bullfinch or other finches in Germany.

We heard today that, as I have said previously, General Paterson is on his way here by way of Purysburg and Two Sisters with the light infantry company of the 71st Scots Regiment, the 2nd Battalion of the same regiment, Ferguson's Corps, the New York Volunteers, the North and South Carolina Provincials, and the dismounted soldiers of the Legion and the 17th Dragoon Regiment, because all the cavalry horses were lost at sea.

The 14th - Colonel Webster received orders to occupy the posts on Stono Ferry with the Jaegers and the 33rd Regiment. Although he was not familiar with the land and because of a scarcity had no guides with him who could speak English, he marched calmly onward with no side patrols and only an advance guard of ten or twelve men, thirty yards ahead of the column. As we emerged from the woods we entered a marshy stretch about 600 to 700 yards long, covered by small, round defensive points which extended to the Stono River. The colonel had ordered a young Negro to lead him to Stono Ferry. However, because the ferry house was on the other side of the river, the Negro thought he wished to cross over. Therefore the whole column marched in this manner without bothering to look around. Suddenly the colonel was aware that rebels occupied the house on the elevated bank on the other side. These were a detachment of Pulaski's Corps, infantry and cavalry, and we were not more than 200 yards from them because the river is very narrow here. In part now there were no boats available to take us across, furthermore, in part, the colonel had no orders to cross. Our rifles were quickly loaded, I think rather too late, and we made a right turn. Fortunately, the rebels had no cannons and were so shocked to suddenly see such an audacious column marching toward them, that they forgot to fire, as they must have thought that possibly a landing had been made at another place and we had arrived here to be transferred across. As we had approached so close and had already passed the above described difficult stretch, and because the morasses could not be avoided, less than half of the Jaeger Detachment was present when the enemy fired on us with grape shot.

This was the unfortunate route where in the previous year the good Colonel [John] Maitland, after so bravely defending the ferry house with 500 to 600 men and two cannons, against 5,000 rebels with six cannons, lost nearly half of his command during his retreat. We pulled back in great haste and remained for a time in the woods. The enemy then burned a small vessel lying in the Stono River to prevent our crossing. During the night the enemy pickets were disturbed and a few cannon shots were fired at the Stono River.

The 15th - The general staff and Engineer Major Moncrief, who had defended Savannah so well, came to reconnoiter the passage. They went more than half way along the swampy road and placed a double jaeger post ahead of them, which the rebels fired upon. Our jaegers also fired a few shots into the enemy house. The engineer wanted to find a dominating height and for this purpose had two English field pieces with him. However, the region on this side of the river was entirely unsatisfactory. At the same time a patrol was sent along the bank to find a shallow crossing place through which to wade. However, because of the deep morass, none was discovered. Toward evening, however, on the upper reaches some old boats were found which the enemy had failed to destroy, and by which means, during the night, several companies of light infantry were transferred across near [Abraham] Watt's house, forcing the rebels to abandon their posts. A Negro who came across the swamp from Charleston brought the report that General Lincoln, with 6,000 to 7,000 men, had gone against General Paterson, and that only during the last few days had work on the defenses been resumed, because the enemy had thought the storm had completely scattered us. Also, no relief force had arrived from General Washington.

The 1st Battalion of Light Infantry marched to Gibbe's house today. Yesterday the army had moved forward near Gibbe's and Wilson's plantations.

The 16th - At noon, as meanwhile our armed boats had pressed forward into the Stono River, the general staff joined us, entered an armed boat, reconnoitered the Stono River initially, and then went ashore to check Wallace's Creek, above which the bridge was broken and whose left bank had been abandoned by the enemy. The Jaeger Detachment, 7th, 23rd, and 71st Regiments, under the command of General Leslie, followed.

This region is the point of land of South Carolina called Stono Many [Mainland ?] and the archipelago St. Andre. I studied the area which Colonel Maitland, as I have already mentioned, defended so valiantly.

The works found here consisted of three quickly constructed redoubts made only of sand, each for 100 men, and three small positions, to the left of the three redoubts, with a hastily constructed, miserable abatis, which altogether formed a half-moon. Both flanks were covered by swamps, but the entire front, at the distance of a musket shot, faced trees which hid the disposition of an attacking force. Almost no tree was left undamaged and five cannonballs had gone through the ferry house.

This is a key position for those who would capture Charleston because it controls the Stono River. Therefore it was a serious mistake for the rebels not to have adequately occupied, or at least to have demolished this position. We immediately began repairs on the two best redoubts.

The 17th - A patrol was sent out to get cattle for the corps and Negroes to work. In so doing they were not aware of any enemy. While I am thinking about the Negroes, I must mention that in the southern part of North America there are a great many. Residents are to be found here who have 200, 300, or even more on their various plantations. They have been purchased in part, and born to other Negroes over time, in part. These people are the laziest in the whole world and must always be driven to work with a whip. Their nourishment consists only of rice and a kind of small brown bean which grows here in abundance. They are clothed only in rags, which barely cover their nakedness and a troop of such variously clad individuals is a comical picture for the German eye. I had a great sympathy for their misery because the Negroes in the northern parts are treated in a completely different manner as to their dress. I therefore asked why the negroes on the land are treated so hard and miserably here, and received this answer. In this province it is reckoned there are about 100 Negroes for every white inhabitant. As they have never attempted to kill all the whites and to take control of the plantations, the inhabitants insure their safety from the insurrection and destruction by employing the whip and fear, which in the northern provinces, where the Negroes are not so numerous, is not necessary.

As the blacks continue to multiply, it will soon no longer be necessary to buy more, if smallpox does not kill off a large number every year.

The 18th - Another patrol was sent out which brought back many cattle. However, as we were far from our ships, without equipment, without guides, without salt, bread, and other foodstuffs, and had only fresh meat and the so-called bread, made of flour and water and cooked in the ashes, to eat, we were not in the best condition.

From a Negro we learned that General Lincoln was some twenty miles the other side of Cox Swamp, near Ponpon.

The 19th - Today a very cold weather, accompanied by frequent rain, set in. Tonight one of our fine row galleys in the Stono River blew up due to the carelessness of two drunken sailors who had a nymph with them. The rebels are working on a fort on the left bank of the Ashley River and the dam which leads here through the deep swamp, in order to fire on one of our landing areas.

The 20th - Today the field artillery and munitions were brought down the Stono River from the fleet in small vessels and then put ashore near Mathew's Ferry. General Huyn's Brigade, which had been at Wilson's plantation, rejoined the army at the Gibbe's and Mathews' Ferry on Johns Island. Three row galleys also went up the river. A patrol of Pulaski's Light Horse reconnoitered our outposts but remained out of range of our rifles.

The 21st - The cold, wet weather continued. Our galleys passed through the channel which joins the Stono River and Wappoo Creek, and entered the Ashley River. Otherwise everything was quiet at our corps.

The 22nd - Our armed boats on the Stono River took two prizes with rice.

Today an officer and eight pioneers went to a house lying about 1,000 yards ahead of our outposts, to sharpen their axes and, without taking the least precaution, enjoyed themselves in complete peace and relaxation. A Negro betrayed them to a patrol of Pulaski's Cavalry riding in the area and they were immediately captured. The 1st Battalion of Light Infantry crossed the Stono River in order to join with Lord Cornwallis' Corps near Gibbe's house.

Tonight a truly winter cold set in which nearly froze not only us, but also the naked Negroes.

The 23rd - It began to snow today and ice formed on the surface of small bodies of water. These two occurrences had never happened previously in this province in the memory of the Negroes.

The patrols which we sent out encountered no enemy. Some patrols went up the Stono River carrying provisions from the fleet to the army.

The 24th - The wind swung around during the night and caused such a sudden change in the weather that by noon today it was as warm here as in Germany on the most beautiful May day.

The army has captured Fort Johnson. This morning the Light Infantry and the English Grenadiers crossed the Stono River near Mathews' Ferry and landed on James Island near Hamilton's landing place.

Before I continue my story, I will briefly describe Johns Island, where the army is now located and at the same time, James Island.

Johns Island, including Wadmalaw Island, is eighteen miles long and ten miles wide. Galleys and schooners can sail around the entire island from the North Edisto River to Stono Inlet. From Stono Inlet to Wappoo Creek even three-masted ships, which carry products of the island to Charleston, can sail. The land is swampy and black ocean soil with many creeks and morasses everywhere. The entire island is covered with pine trees and many cedar woods, through which roadways are cut. The products are rice, indigo, cotton, pitch, and turpentine. In the fields and gardens nothing is found but Indian corn and small brown beans, which the inhabitants call Calabar peas. There are many turkeys in the woods, as well as woodcocks, partridge, and large larks, which are found in an abundance here.

The plantations are well furnished and the owners have six to ten of them. However, from June to the end of September, the owners generally live in the city, because during those months the heat and the insects prevent them from living in the country.

James Island is half as large as Johns Island and, because of the garden produce which grows so well there, is called the garden of Charleston. Some rice and cotton is also grown there.

The 25th - Two patrols, one from Webster's and one from Clarke's Brigades, were sent out again to seize cattle for the army. Captain Cornwallis commanded the first with 100 men, of which I had the honor to command thirty jaegers.

Because I include myself in the description of the patrol's activity, it is necessary that I initially explain to the reader that I do not do this to show my knowledge and cleverness, because here in America similar patrols are the usual duty of every jaeger, but only to give an example of how easily this duty, which after a time one becomes accustomed to, can lead to the loss of honor and reputation.

I placed a non-commissioned officer and six men in the advance guard, a non-commissioned officer and six men in the rear guard, and two men on each side as is generally customary. We had hardly received the report from the advance guard that enemy cavalry had been seen, when the English, in complete disorder, began to run forward so that I had all I could do to hold the captain back until we had a true understanding of the situation. Then I took the rest of the jaegers, in case the advance guard needed support, but the enemy immediately disappeared. Among other items, we captured a wagon loaded with Indian corn and pulled by six oxen, bound for Charleston, as well as the wagon or carriage of the plantation owner where we planned to get the cattle. He had been made aware of our approach by Negroes sent out as outposts, and had sent the cattle into the woods as soon as the advance guard had been seen. However, Colonel Webster kept all of this for himself without giving the smallest portion to the jaegers. Afterward the English captain set fire to the house.

My outposts noticed some militia in the nearby houses; however, they immediately fled. After the cattle had been rounded up and we were about to march back, I asked the captain and his troops to escort the cattle and to allow me to form the rear guard with the thirty jaegers, which he did. I marched with all possible precautions and made frequent halts, first because the patrol was an hour and one-half from the corps, without any support in a region of woods, water, and swamps, where it was necessary to wade up to the knees every thirty yards, and because the enemy was in the vicinity and could easily have cut us off. Fortunately we returned to camp without being attacked. The precautions which I had adopted were very necessary as the second patrol, which had gone out from Clarke's Brigade, had its weapons loaded, as is the British custom, on its return march, but had neither a rear guard nor side patrols, and was followed to one side by Pulaski's Dragoons who attacked in a defile not far from our outposts.

Fortunately, Captain Ewald and his division hurried toward the sound of the shooting and the enemy pulled back after firing a few shots. Nevertheless, the 23rd Regiment suffered seven men wounded in this small patrol and without help would have received far larger losses, in part because the troops were burdened with many fowls, in part because they were escorting many horned cattle, which were difficult to control in the defile.

This afternoon General Leslie returned to Johns Island with the 23rd and 71st Regiments and only the Jaeger Detachment and the 33rd Regiment remained near Stono Ferry under the command of Colonel Webster.

The 26th - After a very cool day yesterday, we had a completely sunny and warm day. Partridge, large larks, and other birds run about our camp, without fear, in great numbers.

Many small boats loaded with munitions, provisions, and baggage for the army pass on the Stono River daily.

The 27th - After Colonel Webster made a small patrol through the woods and nailed placards encouraging Negroes to come into the English lines, the colonel received orders to pull back. He did so this morning. However, because only two small boats were available, crossing the river continued until late at night. On this side the Jaeger Detachment entered camp in a woods an English mile from the ferry near William Ashley's plantation.

However, as we still had to maintain a free passage on the Stono River, a captain and 100 men, including thirty jaegers, were assigned to the two renovated redoubts, without artillery, which is a very dangerous post because the only means of retreat is with two small boats, one of which can only carry fifteen men, or over indescribably bad roads, where it is necessary to withstand fire from the dominating heights without any help. The command is to be relieved every 48 hours. Although Johns Island is completely occupied by us, the boat which was bringing dispatches to Lord Cornwallis was fired upon from the land and a sailor was wounded.

The 28th - The Webster and Clarke Brigades were realigned according to height, which could not be done last night. At noon we heard heavy cannon fire and learned that an enemy row galley had sought to prevent our rebuilding Fort Johnson.

The 29th - Today, with thirty jaegers, I was placed in the detachment of the English Captain Campbell, in the defenses on Stono Many. However, no enemy were seen.

March 1780

The 1st - Yesterday evening many small boats arrived here, which departed again today under the escort of an armed boat. From these we learned that a ship with artillery and munitions had sunk and that the warship *Defiance*, of 64 guns, had run aground on the coast near Tybee Island. During the afternoon a patrol of Pulaski's Cavalry came near our outposts, but as they saw the jaegers run forward to engage them, they quickly withdrew. Tonight an English soldier of the 23rd Regiment deserted his post. This was very disadvantageous for us because thereby the enemy learned that we have no cannons in our positions.

The 2nd - Today the Clarke Brigade rejoined the army. Another enemy patrol appeared before our defenses on Stono Many, but again withdrew after receiving a few rifle shots.

The 3rd - Everything was quiet. We have once again repaired the broken bridge over the Wappoo Creek.

The 4th - This was a very pleasant day for the army because the orders were finally issued for our pay for the previous months of January and February.

The 5th - The general staff was busy reconnoitering James Island and the creeks. Otherwise everything was quiet.

The 6th - As Lieutenant Scheffer was still at headquarters concerning money matters, I had to go to the defenses at Stono Many again. During the evening we received orders, as the Webster Brigade had marched, to await further orders and to be alert as we could not be reinforced.

The 7th - Before daybreak Colonel Webster marched with the Jaeger Detachment and the 33rd Regiment to Mathews' Ferry, where they were transferred across to James Island. Everything was quiet by us.

The 8th - The Light Infantry crossed the Wappoo Bridge to attack 150 enemy dragoons on the right bank of the Ashley River between Drayton's house and the Andrews Bridge. However, as Lieutenant Nash, contrary to orders, had taken his servant, mounted, along with him to pack up the booty, and the servant was seized, the enemy pulled back in time and the lieutenant carried nothing away but a reprimand. Such a strong heat struck Stono Many that the cherry trees began to bloom.

The 9th - At four o'clock this afternoon the order arrived to withdraw as quietly as possible. Shortly thereafter an enemy patrol appeared, which reconnoitered in the woods, out of rifle range, however. At six o'clock the command was transferred across. During this time I patrolled the woods with the jaegers but encountered no enemy. After we had crossed and the boats were destroyed, we marched through the pitch black night until two o'clock in the morning, in a severe storm with much rain, to Mathews' Ferry, where we camped in the huts of the Negroes.

Meanwhile the Jaegers marched over Newtown Cut Bridge today and camped near Scott's house. The Huyn Brigade was near Hamilton's plantation. Not far from Scott's house the English Grenadiers and Clarke's Brigade had their camp; the Hessian Grenadiers were in the region of Fort Johnson; and the Light Infantry was near Hudson's house, where the headquarters was located. The Light Infantry, at the same time, held the bridge over Wappoo Creek.

As I have already mentioned Fort Johnson previously, and the failure of the rebels to occupy it as a serious mistake, I will describe it here.

This fort, destroyed in the previous year by the rebels, was a square with four bastions made of brick, which stood on a hill, completely commanding the harbor. It was designed for 200 men and 24 cannons. At the base of the fort there was a breastwork twelve feet thick, which led along the sandy shore of the harbor. It was constructed of oyster shells and such material piled together, which, as is known, is an impenetrable mass. We built a redoubt for two 24-pounders and two 12-pounders to the left of this fort, which was occupied by a detachment of Hessian Grenadiers.

The 10th - I was transferred across the Stono River, which is very wide here, to James Island and, near Scott's house, joined the rest of the detachment which just then arrived there. We moved forward across Lethusch's plantation, where the headquarters had moved, and entered camp in a woods near Tom Rose's plantation, not far from the Ashley River.

Early this morning Lord Cornwallis passed Wappoo Creek with the Light Infantry. As we and Clarke's Brigade were also across now, posts were established at Linning's and Fenwick's Points in order to control the mouth of Wappoo Creek.

Therefore the army took the following positions: General Leslie and the Light Infantry remained at Linning's Point; the English Grenadiers and Clarke's Brigade at Fenwick's plantation, where Lord Cornwallis had his headquarters; the Webster Brigade was posted at Rose's plantation; the two Hessian Linsing and Lengercke Battalions occupied the post at Hudson's house; and the Jaeger Detachment the road to Ashley Ferry.

The 11th - Everything remained quiet. A deserter from Pulaski's Cavalry came over to us.

The 12th - Today Colonel Abercromby with 500 men of the Light Infantry and two amusettes moved forward to Hammond's house, four miles ahead of the Jaeger's posts to cover a foraging party. Colonel Webster and his brigade marched to the left to protect the flank against [Lieutenant] Colonel [William] Washington, who was in that region with 400 horse. Near Savage's house, a half mile from Rose's house, we encountered a party of twenty horse, which, however, quickly retreated. On our return we laid an ambush, but no enemy appeared.

Yesterday evening work on the third redoubt on Fenwick's Point was begun. A battery for three 32-pounders, two 24-pounders, and one 6-inch howitzer was laid out at Wappoo Creek wharf, which was covered by two round redoubts, each for 300 men, of which the first lay under small arms fire. The enemy fired at our workers today with cannons but without effect, as they were working directly opposite a battery of eight cannons.

The 13th - Once again it was as cold as in winter. We went on patrol but encountered no enemy.

The 14th - Everything remained quiet.

The 15th - During the morning Colonel Fontas [Lieutenant Colonel Thomas Dundas] with 500 men of the Light Infantry marched along the left bank of the Andrews Church Creek, the bridge across which the rebels had destroyed, in order to go foraging. The 33rd Regiment and the jaegers marched toward Loan's plantation.

Toward evening the enemy cavalry was seen near our outposts.

The 16th - Nothing of significance occurred.

The 17th - Captain Hinrichs, as usual, laid an ambush beyond our pickets to prevent the enemy making a close reconnaissance. However, he had already pulled back by ten o'clock. The jaegers had hardly reached the pickets when thirty enemy dragoons appeared and, although they pulled back after some rifle shots, they were able to sneak up on the English pickets and shot a guard in the foot.

The 18th - Captain Ewald had the area ahead of the pickets cut down to make their posts more secure. We also laid an ambush, but no one was seen. The two Hessian battalions, which had been near Fort Johnson, rejoined the army near Hudson's house today. Major [Thomas] Mecan and 120 men were sent to occupy the fort and General Huyn's Brigade was sent forward to Scott's plantation.

Our ships tried to sail father up the Cooper River, but because of too little depth and the entrance being covered by French and American frigates, it was necessary to give up the idea.

The 19th - Everything was quiet by us. We laid out three more redoubts, in the form of a half-circle, on the Ashley River near Linning's house, which are equipped with 24- and 32-pounders. The house was also equipped with a surrounding breastwork and an abatis surrounded all of this. The right side of these entrenchments is on the left bank of the Stono River and the left side, where the old canal enters the Wappoo Creek, in order to cover the provisions fleet in the Stono River.

The 20th - Today a deserter brought the report that General Paterson was nearby. He had acquired horses for the dismounted troops. Our row galleys and armed boats took a position at the entrance to Wappoo Creek, whereupon the enemy frigates near the canal on Sullivan's Island pulled back to the mouth of the Cooper River. Our fleet, except for the warships which lie in the Port Royal River, crossed over the bar between the sandbanks this evening. The guns were unloaded in order to lighten the frigates and then brought up the creek in boats.

The 21st - This evening an enemy dragoon of the Lady Washington's Horse, whose uniform is white with blue facings, fell into our ambush. The man was shot in the knee and his horse in the neck, and he was captured.

The 22nd - This afternoon we were ordered to march. However, we went only four miles and then camped in the woods near the Andrews Church Bridge. The nearby enemy cavalry immediately abandoned their posts. Three companies of light infantry and the Jaegers went one mile beyond the bridge and the morass and took post by the church, where they learned that the enemy had only one forward guard in the outpost. We are now one mile from Ashley Ferry.

The 23rd - This morning a command of light infantry and jaegers moved to Drayton's house, which was the headquarters for General Leslie. As the bridge over the Andrews Creek was finished, the general staff wished to reconnoiter under cover of the jaeger pickets, which I had the good fortune to command today. The Hessian Grenadiers entered the Webster camp near Rose's house and occupied the Andrews Bridge and a portion of the bank near Ashley's Ferry. The Jaeger Detachment camped near Drayton's house.

The 24th - The Light Infantry, 33rd Regiment, and Jaegers made a patrol to Middleton's and the Rack's plantations, seven miles beyond our posts, from which we learned that Colonel Washington and his cavalry had crossed the Ashley River and occupied Bacon's Bridge. Today, for the first time since our landing, we saw the first hill, but still no stones.

The 25th - An enemy patrol approached to reconnoiter, but remained at a great distance. The army drew closer together and the general staff reconnoitered the Ashley River.

The 26th - A sergeant-major of the Virginia Light Horse, which wears a green and red uniform like the Hessian Jaegers, approached too near the Jaeger picket, fell into one of our ambushes, was shot through the body, and died during the night.

General Paterson crossed over Randolph's [Rantowle's] Creek, which lies nine miles from Drayton's plantation and seven miles from Ashley Ferry. The general wanted to visit him to inspect his corps and the 400 riders. They had withdrawn only an hour when Colonel [John] Hamilton and an English doctor, who were also returning to the army, were captured by rebels who had hidden in the woods, as no one had thought to protect this road. Therefore it was only luck that prevented the generals, accompanied by only six cavalrymen, from experiencing the same misfortune.

The 27th - The mounted and foot soldiers of the Legion, from General Paterson's Corps, crossed over to us.

As we were now masters of most of the Ashley River, and Charleston lies between it and the Cooper River, the general-in-chief made all necessary preparations to transport the army across. To this end we received, on

The 28th - orders to be ready to march. The army drew ever closer together and General Paterson also joined us. During the night our flatboats sneaked past the enemy batteries, using muffled oars, and gathered at Wappoo Creek, where it enters the Ashley River and where our row galleys lay.

The 29th - At eight o'clock in the morning we marched to Drayton's house, which lies on the Ashley River. Here, where sixty to eighty flatboats were assembled, we joined the Light Infantry.

The embarkation order was as follows, namely:

1) Light Infantry, 2 battalions under General Leslie
2) Jaeger Detachment, Major von Wurmb
3) Hessian Grenadiers, 4 battalions, General von Kospoth
4) English Grenadiers, 2 battalions, Lieutenant Colonel Abercromby
5) 7th and 23rd Regiments, Colonel Clarke
6) 33rd and 71st Regiments, Colonel Webster
7) One squadron of the 17th Dragoon Regiment.

Lord Cornwallis commanded the landing; Agent Captain Tonken the embarkation, and Captain Elphinstone the crossing.

The Jaegers were withdrawn from Webster's Brigade on the orders of the general-in-chief and are to perform duty only with the Light Infantry. The two battalions of light infantry and the jaegers were embarked alone and sailed to the left up the Ashley River, under the escort of an armed boat. After a voyage of about four English miles, we were aware of a possible landing site on the opposite, slightly raised bank, by Benjamin Fuller's house, as the other bank was covered with swamp and reeds. As our armed boat saw a double cavalry post at this house and we did not know it the enemy had cannons there, our boats had to wait briefly. The armed boat sailed forward and fired on the cavalry post, which together with pickets hidden behind the house, returned the fire. When we saw that there were no cannons there, our boats sailed to the shore and the men sprang ashore so quickly, with the usual English ardor, that in ten minutes everyone was ashore and had formed a half-moon around the house. This region is called the Muck and is fourteen miles from Charleston.

As Captain Hinrichs was on the other side with the picket, I had the honor to command the division.

Captain Ewald was sent ahead a short distance with some men to establish forward posts and skirmished with enemy dragoons observing us.

The equipment and heavy cannons had to be left behind due to a shortage of boats and only the Light Infantry's two light field cannon accompanied us. As no more of the enemy were encountered, we halted until the remaining troops were transferred across. After this occurred the army marched along the road from Dorchester to Charleston, which appeared like an uninterrupted way. The Jaeger Detachment served as the advance guard for the army. After a march of about six miles, we camped in a woods close to the road we traveled. On the march the enemy cavalry rode constantly ahead of us, but remained out of range of our rifles. The night was quiet. We only saw, from a distance toward the water, a picket of Negroes.

During the landing Colonel Tarleton made a patrol toward Dorchester with 200 mounted men. Colonel Washington, however, received reports of this and occupied Bacon's Bridge over the Ashley River.

As the army now advanced on Charleston, General Paterson had to occupy the redoubts at Fenwick's Point and near Linning's house on James Island, in order to cover communications between the transport ships lying in the Stono River, near Hudson's house, and the army.

The 30th - Was a hot day for the jaegers. I have already said that the Jaeger Detachment formed the army's advance guard and from these a captain with sixty men was sent on ahead. We had just passed the Governor's House, about four miles outside Charleston, when several shots were fired by our advance guard at some enemy cavalry who had come too close and of whom one man was killed. Shortly thereafter the firing increased. Three hundred rebels, consisting of light infantry and Negroes, had lain an ambush along both sides of the road, in the woods, and had a small defensive position behind them to cover their retreat. Therefore they gave our advance guard a warm reception. The general staff, which was following close behind on horses, halted and the remainder of the Jaeger Detachment rushed forward to support the advance guard. This took place with such swiftness and ardor that in less than fifteen minutes, despite the morass before us, that was difficult to pass, and despite our being only 200 men, the enemy was driven into flight. We then halted on orders from the general because the region here was in the form of a defile and no one could tell whether or not the enemy had cannons supporting them. Also, the rebels had placed our mounted general staff, which had halted, in danger, and shot the Earl of Caithness in the upper body while he was halted beside the general-in-chief. As a company of light infantry then moved forward to cover our left flank and fired several shots from one of their field pieces at those in flight, the enemy abandoned the position which the advance guard immediately occupied. It had been the enemy commander's intention to draw us before his cannons during the heat of battle. However, as they gave way, we also withdrew from the trap, so they reentered their position. They remained there only a few minutes and then made their retreat. We took this opportunity to fire a number of rifle shots after them, which hastened their evacuation. The general-in-chief personally expressed his thanks to the Jaegers for their demonstration of bravery during the skirmish. One jaeger had been lightly wounded and one was missing.

During the affair we learned how important it is to be familiar with a region. If we had not had a thorough knowledge of this area, it would have been easy for the enemy to have cut off our detachment beyond the Black Creek dam during the skirmish. As it was, we were not hindered during our withdrawal.

After the affair the army camped near the Governor's House so that the right wing rested on the Ashley River and the left wing on the Cooper River. The Jaeger Detachment moved to the right wing and camped in the woods near Gibbe's Creek. Colonel Webster, with the 33rd and 71st Regiments, covered the army's rear and the Light Infantry occupied a small defensive position. The headquarters was located at Wilson's house on the left wing. Everything was quiet during the night.

The 31st - The jaeger picket moved forward to the woods and morass near the Gibbe's house, so that the general staff and Engineer Major Moncrief could be protected while the defensive works, which extended beyond the Black River dam, could be reconnoitered and the city and its defenses, from which we were about a mile and one-quarter, could be observed from an empty house.

As can best be determined from here, the Charleston defenses are laid out in the form of a half-moon and 57 gun embrasures can be counted along the front.

I must note here, however, that the otherwise so clever Moncrief initially misjudged the distance by 400 yards, as we later determined, when laying out the batteries. This error was apparently caused by the city's defenses being somewhat elevated.

According to people with knowledge of such things, the siege will take much time and effort, because:

1st - The defenses are considerable and in good condition

2nd - The enemy has far more artillery than we have

3rd - We must first make ourselves masters of Sullivan's Island, which has a strong fort protecting its troops

4th - We must clear the French and American frigates out of our way, and

5th - We must bring all the cannons and munitions in boats, through the creeks, from James Island and because of a shortage of horses and equipment, move them into the trenches with the help of blacks and sailors.

April 1780

The 1st - The Ashley River was crossed with dificulty, from Linning's Creek to Gibbe's Ferry, yesterday and today, and then onward to the park at Gibbe's house. The Negroes moved the cannons, munitions, and provisions up, and the green house was converted to laboratory. All the wooden houses in this region were then torn down and made into a new sort of mantelet by Major Moncrief. They were made of timbers and boards, six feet high and twelve to fourteen feet long, and provided with three base supports to hold them upright. These were used to construct batteries and redoubts. The fascines and straw sides were quickly completed. As soon as the engineers had set them together, the shapes of the battery or redoubt was finished and the workers then threw dirt from the trenches upon them. This method is very practical, but only possible in sandy and soft soil.

Today the missing jaeger was found in the underbrush by the river. In examining him it was discovered that he had been killed by three bullets and his death posture indicated that he had prayed for forgiveness.

During the night we began our work. Thereupon 1,500 workers and a covering force of Colonel Abercromby with the Light Infantry and 500 grenadiers commanded by Lieutenant Colonels Webster and [Otto Christian Wilhelm] von Linsing was sent out. The station for the covering force as well as for the workers was on the road from Dorchester to Charleston, at the spot where the road from Gibbe's house intersected. To the right a redoubt forty yards wide was to be constructed, 200 yards farther another of similar size, and at a farther distance to the left, another of eighty yards was to be laid out. For communications, or better said, to the first parallel, which is 800 yards from the enemy lines, a three foot deep ditch, which the rebels had forgotten to fill-in, is used. The entire work extended about 600 yards. During the night the enemy hardly fired a dozen cannon shots and gave not the slightest indication of disturbing our work.

The 2nd - Today we worked very hard transporting cannons and finishing the mantelets. We already had five 24-pounders and two 6-inch howitzers in the gun park. As a ship with artillery had been lost from the fleet and there was a serious shortage of cannons, the cannons from the warships *Raisonnable* and *Europa*, lying in the Port

Royal River, were brought here under the direction of Captain [Henry Francis] Evans, so that they could be used during the siege. The rebels fired individual shots this afternoon with a 24-pounder against our works. The jaeger picket was withdrawn again to Gibbe's house. We awaited a 2,000 man reinforcement from New York. During the night the already started parallels and redoubts were improved. The enemy fired only a little.

The 3rd - The work on the mantelets, the transporting of cannons, and the improvements to the parallels were continued with the greatest possible speed. The enemy fired occasionally and threw random 6-inch bombs into our works, wounding two Hessian grenadiers. During the night two new redoubts were begun, each laid out in the form of a half-moon; one to the right near the Ashley River for about 200 men, and to the left, close to the right bank of the Cooper River, on a small height, for nine heavy cannons. Both were 100 yards closer to the enemy. They were not protected from the enemy, however, who fired only against the first parallel.

The 4th - As an attack was expected, Major von Wurmb, with 160 jaegers, was ordered to occupy the redoubt on the right at daybreak and Captain Ewald, with sixty jaegers, the one on the left, in order to support the troops occupying the same. The latter redoubt had no communications trench. Therefore two Hessian field pieces were hidden therein. At daybreak the enemy cannonaded both redoubts and at nine o'clock two French frigates, which had lain before the city, fired on the left redoubt. However, they were forced to withdraw by fire from two 24-pounders and an howitzer 'which had been hurriedly placed 400 yards behind the redoubt, near the distillery. At six o'clock in the evening an enemy schooner, which fired into the rear of the redoubt, approached, but then laid at anchor with two frigates, three miles higher up the Cooper River, opposite the Governor's House. The rebels did not direct their bombs poorly. One of them fell in the left redoubt between two powder kegs for the Hessian field pieces, just in front of the general-in-chief and Lord Cornwallis. This heavy cannonade, nevertheless, was only twelve shots into the breastworks, and the entire loss consisted on one dead and one seriously wounded Englander and two slightly wounded Hessian grenadiers. During the night our works were improved. The enemy fired heavily at the workers. The Jaeger Detachment was divided into three sections. The first remained in camp, the other two settled on either side, to the left and to the right, of the main road.

The 5th - Today there was a heavy cannonade. This evening our battery near the distillery also began to fire toward the Cooper River to clear it of enemy ships. As the general-in-chief wished to show the rebels that our preparations were completed and we were ready to burn the city down, he allowed the two redoubts constructed by us across the Ashley River on James Island, at Fenwick's Point and near Linning's house, to fire into the city for two hours. At the same time our two row galleys lying at the mouth of Wappoo Creek opened fire with heated-shot, setting some houses on fire. The rebels were so astonished by this compliment that during the entire time they fired not a single shot.

Two hundred sailors moved into the works to help handle the cannons. During the night a battery of nine 24-pounders was set up in the first parallel, on our right wing, between redoubts one and two. These guns were manned by the sailors.

The 6th - At four o'clock this afternoon the rebels resumed firing. A special type of large flatboat, which was to be armed with two 6-pounders, was brought on wheels from the Ashley to the Cooper River to drive the enemy boats, which had withdrawn from the city during the night and then anchored on the bank of the Cooper River, farther up the river.

The Legion crossed the Ashley River today, as they were transferred to Webster's Brigade from Paterson's Corps. During the night a 150-yard long communications trench was completed between numbers 5 and 6. It was planned to put heavy cannons in Number 6. However, as the swampy road leading there was neither wide nor level, nor paved with logs, and had not been checked, the cannons became bogged down. The enemy batteries fired heavily today but were answered with a lively fire from James Island.

Because a deserter who came in during the night said that the rebels planned to make a sortie at daybreak, the Light Infantry was immediately ordered into the trenches with the orders to mix in among the enemy as much as possible and in this manner to enter the city. For this reason, each was to tie a white cloth around his head so that he could be differentiated in the darkness. However, the rebels did not make a sortie.

The 7th - The enemy again fired rather heavily. However, the sailor's battery, which greatly distinguished itself throughout the siege, did its duty and, when so ordered, fired many heated shots into the city. About one o'clock in the afternoon eleven sloops and schooners with troops passed down the Cooper River into the city. It was a reinforcement from Washington and consisted of about 600 men. The rebels raised a great victory cry and throughout the night rang the bells amidst a continuous cannon fire.

We were also no less joyful, because Captain [Robert] Collins arrived with eighty English artillerymen, who were much needed. He had been separated from the fleet during the storm and just when his ship was about to sink, he was saved by an English privateer. He was taken to Bermuda initially and then brought here.

During the night the enemy fired a heavy cannonade; nevertheless, a redoubt for six large cannons was constructed in the form of a half-moon, which the enemy failed to discover. This brought the enemy defenses 200 yards closer and four 24-pounders were immediately placed in redoubt Number 6. The armed boat was placed in the water and the Light Infantry cleared an enemy double outpost from ahead of the abatis. By this means it was accidently learned that during the first skirmish with the Jaegers on 31 March, the enemy had suffered one captain, one lieutenant, one sergeant, and seven men killed, and General Lincoln's adjutant and twenty men wounded. Those heavy losses were the reason that no mercy was shown to any stray jaeger.

Before I continue, I will mention serious consequences can result from a small error during a war.

If the engineer, as I have mentioned, had previously reconnoitered the swampy road to the redoubt and made the necessary repairs, redoubt Number 6, which borders on the Cooper River, could have been provided with heavy cannons yesterday evening, or at least this morning, by which means the sloops carrying the enemy reinforcements could have been given a warm reception. As it was, we patiently watched the vessels sail past us in the rain.

The 8th - This was a memorable day. The navy had planned to come to the aid of the army by firing a cannonade from the water, or possibly making a landing. Although the inhabitants of Sullivan's Island, who by means of Fort Moultrie had blockaded the harbor, appeared too annoying and too dangerous, it was decided nevertheless to pass this region of enemy fire and many sandbanks. Therefore, this afternoon Admiral Arbuthnot fortunately led a fleet consisting of fourteen sail, frigates and armed transport ships, past an exceptionally heavy cannonade from Fort Moultrie, and dropped anchor between the fort and the city. His losses consisted of seven dead and twenty seriously wounded. The second ship, the frigate *Richmond*, lost its masts and an armed transport ship, after its cargo was removed, was set on fire during the night because it had run aground on a sandbank.

As audacious and as fortunate as this undertaking was, it was not necessary. The admiral had forgotten to ask if the way from Sullivan's Island to the city was open and if it were possible to attack the defenses from the water side, successfully. However, he found the channel so well blockaded by nine sunken ships that it was impossible to approach closer to the city and the batteries were so placed that he could not attack them. Nevertheless, the rebels were so shaken by the audacious undertaking against their fortress that during the night and on

The 9th - their batteries were almost unheard. The inhabitants were so shocked that they took their finest belongings to the left bank of the Cooper River and retreated out of the city. During the night a battery of six cannons was laid out 300 yards ahead of the parallel between Numbers 4 and 5, and strenuous efforts made to place large cannons therein.

In considering Gibbe's house, where our artillery park, powder magazines, and laboratories were located, I found sufficient reason to moan about the English carelessness. At every camp site in the world, it is customary in those places where cannons and munitions are, to have a guard and especially to place a double guard on the laboratory to prevent all individuals who have no official business from entering, because an enemy plot or other carelessness can cause the powder to blow up or the cannons to be spiked, which could possibly destroy the entire camp. However, the English not only allow everyone to enter the park, but even the deserters, who as a rule are kept under close observation and at a distance from the camp, were to be seen at the magazine and in the trenches, even though we had reason because of our few cannons to be careful and because of a shortage of munitions were often restricted during the day to firing only three shots an hour, and the soldiers were given a reward of half an English shilling for every cannonball they recovered.

To tell the truth, the English must credit the advantage achieved by their weapons, not to good conduct, or their precautions, but only to blind luck and the mistakes of the rebels.

The 10th - As the Engineer Major Moncrief saw that it was not possible to silence the enemy cannons with his weapons, and had decided therefore to capture the city by digging only saps in sandy soil, it was necessary to have a well-directed and limited fire to cover the workers. Therefore today one captain, one lieutenant, and sixty jaegers were sent into the trenches to accomplish this purpose. The enemy cannonade was very lively today, but the frigates continued to lie at anchor near the city. At six o'clock in the evening the general-in-chief, through Major Crosbie, called upon the city to surrender, but received as an answer that sixty days had passed before he, General Lincoln, was aware that General Clinton intended to take hostile action against the city. As he no longer had any doubts, however, he would wait to see what would happen.

The third armed boat was brought into the Cooper River. During the night work continued on the previously begun batteries and communications trenches, from the first parallel to this one, and weapons were placed in the finished positions. The enemy interrupted this work frequently with cannon fire and bombs, which firing continued on

The 11th - until four o'clock in the morning. This was answered only by our battery at Fenwick's Point. During this night work progressed on a demi place d'armes, 200 yards long, extending on each side of the forward battery. The enemy sought to hinder this work with a heavy cannon and musket fire.

The 12th - At four o'clock this afternoon a frigate and three armed brigantines, without firing a shot, passed Fort Moultrie under a heavy enemy fire and joined the fleet. Two deputations from North Carolina came to the army today with offers to raise 1,000 armed men if they were protected by English weapons.

As the rebels still held the land on the other side of the Cooper River and the general-in-chief feared that General Lincoln would retreat from the city with the garrison at night, Lieutenant Colonel Webster was sent along the Dorchester Road on the right bank of the

Ashley River with the 33rd Regiment, the Legion, and Ferguson's Corps, in order to cross the Cooper River and cut the rebel communications and to force the abandonment of his defenses on Lempriere's Point.

During the night a mortar battery was begun in the demi place d'armes to the left of the previously laid out battery.

The 13th - As our batteries were now equipped with twenty-one 24-pounders, two 12-pounders, and one mortar, they opened fire at nine-thirty in the morning. They were fortunate in that they destroyed an enemy cannon with the first twenty shots. Some shells were fired also from Number 6, which fell on one or another of the outer parts of the city and set fire to some houses. This resulted in a heavy cannonade by both sides. During the evening the 64th Regiment crossed the Ashley River in order to join with Webster's Corps. Tonight our cannon fire was heavier than the enemy's because they were working on changes to their embrasures. We made our approach according to a system called a double sap, from the right hand of the first parallel, left from Number 2 and from the demi place d'armes outward about 130 yards, without any hindrance from the enemy. The 23rd Regiment followed Webster's Corps so as to cover the rear of the corps.

The 14th - The previously begun work was continued during the day. While this progressed, the enemy remained inactive. During the night the second parallel was opened. The enemy tried to prevent this with grape and small arms fire.

The 15th - The enemy cannonade was very strong again and ours, on the other hand, somewhat weaker. The enemy galleys, which lay near Lempriere's Point, approached close to the shore, not far from the Governor's House, and fired on the Hessian Grenadiers' camp. Thereupon a battery of 24-pounders was quickly thrown up and forced the galleys to withdraw to their former station. Today we also received the welcome report that a few days ago, Colonel Tarleton, with his cavalry, had attacked Colonel Washington near Bacon's Bridge. About thirty dragoons, including Major [Pierre Francois] Vernier, the commandant of Pulaski's Corps, were killed and sixty dragoons and 200 horses, as well as equipment, were captured. Colonel Washington, who was wounded and captured, escaped into the water. As a result of this affair, Pulaski's Corps ceased to exist.

As small as this affair appears to have been, it is very important to us as it assured our occupation of Bacon's Bridge over the Cooper River, made Colonel Webster master of many provisions, and cleared the way to move closer to the Wando River, placing him in a position to cut all communications with the city by way of the Cooper River. As a further hindrance to all communications with the city on the river, several armed ships were posted in Servan Bay and others in Spencer's Inlet.

During the night we began saps in two places from the second parallel. The enemy did little firing but had made a contra-approach between his first and second abatis, to allow his ruffians to fire upon our jaegers.

The 16th - Today our bomb battery, containing twenty royals and coehorns, fired frequently at the enemy with grape shot. The battery of four 24-pounders on James Island, established by the admiral, was opened today also. Toward evening an enemy row galley moved closer to the bank on this side of the Cooper River, fired on the English hospital, and wounded a man who was sick. However, it was forced to withdraw by a hastily brought up Hessian field piece. Thereafter a 24-pounder was placed before the house. During the night the previously begun approaches were extended and widened under a heavy enemy fire.

The 17th - Today the prisoners taken by Colonel Tarleton were delivered to the army. As the breastworks to our approaches were still not strong enough and the traverses were too few, the enemy cannon fire did much damage to us. Despite this, our bomb batteries did not fire until the jaeger captain in the trenches, through the commanding staff officer, forced the artillery officer, toward evening, to fire his weapons. A jaeger was wounded by a cannonball today. During the night a demi place d'armes was laid out 300 yards from the second parallel on both flanks of the approaches.

The 18th - As we continued our work during the day, the enemy fired heavily with grape and small arms and also fired many bombs. They continued a similar fire during the night because we were working on the communications lines of the second parallel.

The 19th - Small mortars were brought to the demi place d'armes, and the second parallel and the approaches opened. We threw many grenades and bombs into the enemy's defenses today and were only

450 yards from the fortress. At the same time we received the most welcome news that after an eleven day voyage, a fleet with a 2,600-man reinforcement, artillery, and munitions had arrived from New York. The troops on board consisted of the 42nd English Regiment and the Hessian Ditfurth Infantry Regiment, the Brunswick Corps, Volunteers of Ireland, the Queen's Rangers, and some New York militia. With these reinforcements we were finally in a condition now to close off Charleston.

The king of the Lower Creek Indians, who had been told that our army was in very bad condition in order to get his nation away from supporting the English, came to us. On orders of the general-in-chief he was shown about the camp and in the trenches. He appeared to have a sort of brown color, wore rings in his nose and in his slit ears, spoke only a little English, and otherwise his behavior was that of a manly individual. He had a 78-year old Scot with him, as a companion, who had lived among this nation since 1748. The Scot was as spry and alert as a man of forty years. He is Colonel [William] McIntosh, who in the last rebellion in 1746 in his native land had belonged to the party of the Pretender and had commanded the left wing of the army at the Battle of Culloden. He was now the most loyal subject of the King [of England].

As we approached on the left tonight, the enemy directed a heavy cannon and bomb fire, which our bomb positions and batteries on James Island answered effectively.

The 20th - Our jaegers worked wonders. The enemy batteries were now so close that they flanked the trenches and an Ansbach jaeger behind the sandbags was killed by a cannonball. Thereafter the jaegers, by their excellent rifle fire, kept the enemy's embrasures silent throughout the day. Several of our bombs also exploded two of the enemy's powder magazines. The troops who arrived from New York were landed today near Hamilton's landing on James Island.

The approaches were extended even farther during the night, and in the second parallel,, on the main road, a battery for three 6-pounders was laid out under a strong enemy cannonade, which we countered only with bombs.

The 21st - During the afternoon General Lincoln sent a flag of truce to our general-in-chief, offering to capitulate, and suggested to this end a six-hour armistice, which last, with the agreement of

Admiral Arbuthnot, was accepted. Later, however, after the rebels had requested, among other conditions, freedom to pull out of the city and that they not have to surrender as prisoners of war, the state of hostilities was resumed at ten o'clock.

Thereafter we continued to enter our approaches on the left and right and laid out two demi place d'armes, each about 150 yards long.

The 22nd - The rebels showed by an exceptionally heavy cannonade throughout the day, that they were angry at our rejection of the capitulation. We also suffered many dead and wounded. A jaeger was among the dead. Despite the losses we continued our work during the night with such zeal that we approached within six yards of the enemy's first abatis.

The 23rd - The cannonade by both sides was not as strong. Colonel Webster and his corps have already reached Coinghook [Cainhoy ?] and the 42nd Regiment, Queen's Rangers, and the Volunteers of Ireland rejoined the army.

During the night our only efforts were toward improving the positions which had been severely damaged by the enemy cannonade of yesterday.

The 24th - Captain Hinrichs and Lieutenant von Winzingerode moved out as usual and entered the trenches before daybreak.

The rebels made an attack from their left wing against the work on our right, in which were Lieutenant von Winzingerode with thirty jaegers, and an officer and fifty men of the Light Infantry.

As the English, until daybreak when they saw the jaegers coming, occupied the post in their usual manner but without loaded weapons or fixed bayonets, and had not been especially alert, they were not aware of the rebels until they sprang over the breastwork. The Light Infantry, who were neither on guard nor able to fire against the enemy, ran away so that Lieutenant von Winzingerode was forced to retreat. At that time four jaegers, including one Ansbacher, were allowed to return. During this confusion, it would have been easy for the rebels to ruin our bomb battery, which was nearby, but as soon as our second parallel began to fire, they ran away so quickly that their troops left thirteen muskets and two hats on the ground before our position.

During the day the enemy fire was continuous, as usual. During the night approaches were opened up to the edge of the enemy's trenches, and along the same. The third parallel was opened also, despite the rebels firing heavily with grape and small arms.

About twelve o'clock the rebels pulled back to their abatis and shouted, "Avances! Tires!" while still delivering a continuous fire by platoons.

The 25th - As our troops were still thinking about yesterday's rebel attack, they thought the rebels were attacking again. Therefore the workers ran from the trenches and the covering force fell back, some in good order, some not in good order. The second parallel occupants, who thought our retreating troops were enemies, fired upon them, killing one Scottish officer, four Scottish soldiers, and two Hessian grenadiers. Twelve English and two Hessians were wounded. About one o'clock the error was noticed. No rebels had come beyond the abatis, and furthermore, at daybreak they pulled back from the first abatis. We fired a bomb after them as revenge. If the rebels had been smart and daring, what could they have accomplished in this situation!

After the general-in-chief had been strengthened by the reinforcement from New York, and as Colonel Webster with his troops could not cover all the approaches, Lord Cornwallis crossed the Cooper River with the Volunteers from Ireland and the North and South Carolina militia in our armed boats and some captured boats, in order to join with Colonel Webster and took over command. This opportunity enabled us to capture an enemy schooner with six cannons, loaded with rum and rice, which had grounded firmly on the shore on that side, and was awaiting the flood tide. Today General Paterson, with the 63rd Regiment, rejoined the army while Colonel [Max von] Westerhagen, with the Ditfurth Regiment and the Brunswick Corps, occupied the batteries on James Island.

The 26th - Improvements were made on the works begun the previous night and the third parallel, and three batteries were laid out. Our bomb battery fired with good effect today, but we also suffered some troop losses, including one Hessian jaeger, due to enemy fire.

As obvious as it was that ships could not draw nearer to the city, Admiral Arbuthnot planned, because a favorable wind blew today, to attack the city from the water side. We were also fully prepared to storm the city. With this end in view the Light Infantry moved into the trenches. However, the entrance was so completely blocked with sunken ships, that nothing developed from the plan.

The night was used to complete the three previously begun batteries and to lay our several traverses in order to counter the enemy's flanking fire. At the same time to the left of the second parallel, with the help of our bombs, and despite a heavy enemy cannonade, a battery for two 6-pounders was begun.

The enemy set three fires between his abatis, which he kept burning all night. Despite the fact that this light created danger to our workers, no one gave it any heed, neither worrying about it when lit nor while being maintained, but which certainly should have been noticed because of the small arms fire alone.

The 27th - Both sides fired heavily and the work on the trenches was continued in earnest. During the night the battery on the left of the second parallel was almost completed, although the enemy had tried to prevent it with a constant musket fire, which caused the batteries on either side to be engaged throughout the night.

The 28th - We put mortars in the third parallel because, of all of our cannons, we had only two 24-pounders in Number 6.

We could not use more for fear of damaging our own works, which a few days previous we could not have said about our cannonade.

For some time we had moved the batteries forward as work on the parallels moved forward, until moving the batteries farther would have been of no value.

The demi place d'armes between the second and third parallels was moved toward the main dam so that we could destroy the sluice and drain the water from the enemy canal.

The 29th - We worked during the day on the new approach, which drew considerable bomb and small arms fire upon us. The cannons were almost completely silenced by the rifle fire of our jaegers. Only one jaeger was wounded by a piece of a bomb, as the entrance and exit march by the jaegers was very dangerous when the cannons fired on the pathways. Today we received the most pleasant report that the rebels had vacated the defenses on Lempriere's Point and retreated into the city. Lord Cornwallis immediately occupied the position. We took four cannons, much ammunition, and a number of small ships. With the loss of this post, the rebels have lost all possibility of retreating overland.

During the night work on the second and third parallels was strenuously pushed and the approach reached so close to the dam that it was possible to shoot over the edge of the trenches, despite the enemy cannon fire which was continuous and heavy.

The 30th - The enemy batteries were again quiet. Our workers were divided so that 200 entered the trenches during the day and 200 at night. The forces occupying our combined positions at that time amounted to 1,200 men. During the night the batteries were furnished with ammunition, and clearing the canal was begun.

May 1780

The 1st - Today it was possible to notice how much the water in the canal had been lowered by last night's work. The enemy cannon fire was as heavy today as it had been during the previous night. One jaeger lost his right hand due to the cannon fire and another was killed by a musket ball. This evening about 200 men occupied the first parallel and the remaining 1,000 men the second and third parallels. Our bomb battery silenced the enemy fire. The work tonight was the same as yesterday. This produced a heavy musket fire from the rebels, which we answered only with bombs.

The 2nd - Our deserters, according to enemies who have come over to us, have betrayed the times when the jaegers go in and out of the trenches. As the jaegers are very much disliked because of the great losses inflicted by their rifles, the enemy has set up four cannons to the left and right which can fire across the route leading into the trenches. Two hours before daylight and two hours after sunset, they fire their cannonballs which we can not avoid during our entrance and exit. The enemy small arms fire was very heavy today and wounded one of our jaegers.

The 3rd - Although it was Captain Hinrichs turn to occupy the trenches with a lieutenant and sixty jaegers, nevertheless, on the orders of Major von Wurmb, I had the honor to command both posts with this force. To protect myself from the frequent cannonballs, I marched out a little earlier than usual and halted at the first parallel until it was daylight. Still, a cannonball fell on the edge of the trench where we paused, so close that we were covered with sand. Also, in passing the swamp made by the tide en route to the second parallel, we had to tolerate more cannonballs. Although during the day we had to repair the weak breastwork of the third parallel, which had been seriously damaged during the night, the enemy cannon fire was not as heavy and was easily silenced by the jaegers. We approached so close to the enemy abatis with our sap that in places we could touch it with our hand. As we now had to protect ourselves while working so close, we had to lay out sandbags which drew a concentrated musket fire against us. When we left this position we were fired on with cannons once again, but without suffering the least harm.

During the night work on the approach already started from the right of the small position for firing on the enemy continued so that now the water ran out from it in a stream. The enemy fired heavily with cannons and muskets.

The 4th - When Captain Bodungen marched into the trenches, one of the incoming cannonballs fell among his troops, blew one jaeger's foot off, and wounded four others. Also during the day the rebels fired continuously, killing one jaeger. Lord Cornwallis sent in twenty captives, including Captain [Edward] Rutledge, a son of the governor of Charleston. Our armed boats captured a three-masted ship lying at anchor in the middle of the Cooper River, not far from the city. There were sick Negroes on board. The 64th Regiment came back from Lord Cornwallis. The enemy cannonade during the night was so strong that our workers could not work very much.

The 5th - The rebels made a contra-approach from their left wing last night, which flanked ours, and continued working on it today. The jaegers sought to prevent this but in part the enemy were already too deep in the earth, in part they protected their workers with 100 men, against whom we could employ only a few jaegers because the others were engaged against the embrasures.

During the night work proceeded on completing the mining of the canal and on the third parallel.

The 6th - Today the enemy fired very little. However a smart Englishman was found during the bombing. Since we began work on the third parallel many troops have been killed and wounded by fire from an empty old house lying between the two enemy abatis, without anyone exerting the necessary effort to destroy it. Finally today, an artillery officer was able to get close enough to set it on fire.

During the night the enemy fire from cannons and small arms was continuous. In the defenses, as well as in the city, everything was in motion. Apparently they had been advised to burn the old houses thinking we were about to storm the city. Toward this end we had completed the necessary preparations for opening the second and third parallels. They were equipped with 23 guns, 2 howitzers, and 22 mortars, of which one was 13-inches. The rebels continued their firing during the night although we had disrupted it.

The 7th - Because the enemy fire against us when marching into the trenches was exceptionally strong, we allowed only three men to move at a time to prevent a serious loss. The breastwork for the third parallel, which had caved in considerably due to the powerful cannonade and the heavy rain, was improved under a heavy enemy musket fire, which our jaegers countered effectively. Our bomb batteries silenced the enemy ones toward evening but only after a jaeger was killed.

The captain of a transport ship wished to visit the trenches as he desiring learning from whence the cannonballs came. However, he had hardly raised his head above the parapet before a ball hit him dangerously in the head. When reproached for his curiosity, he said, "I did not believe that it is so dangerous for a person to take only a quick glance."

We heard some significant signals on the Cooper River and learned that when Admiral Arbuthnot sought to correct his mistake, he had decided to capture Fort Moultrie. To this end he had made landings at two places, early in the evening, and, according to reports, when few sailors were on the island. The occupants of a detached defensive position were attacked and captured. The fort was called upon to surrender. As the commandant saw that the sailors and marines had landed on the eastern shore and were prepared to attack, he surrendered and with his 150 men was made a prisoner of war. We also captured twenty cannons in the fort. The sailors made fun of the poor defense as the rebels marched out and, instead of weapons, held oars in their hands.

At the same time the best of news was received. Colonel Tarleton had attacked the enemy cavalry on the Santee River, cut down many, and captured forty men. This incident developed in the following manner. Lord Cornwallis sent Lieutenant [Lovett] Ashe [of the 38th Regiment of Foot] with a detachment of mounted light infantry on a reconnaissance to Lenud's Ferry. As that officer did not take the necessary precautions, he was cut off by the rebels and captured. Therefore Lord Cornwallis sent Colonel Tarleton with the Legion in pursuit of the enemy, consisting of cavalry commanded by Colonels Washington and White. Tarleton overtook them near Lenud's Ferry, attacked with his usual spirit, routed the entire force, and captured 100 horses. The two colonels barely escaped, making a dangerous swim across the wide Santee River. Most of the remaining troops drowned, part in the river and part remained stuck in the swampy banks of the river.

Lieutenant Ashe, who was already in a boat with his troops, waiting to be transferred across the river, seeing his rescuers on the bank, threw the guards into the water and joined with Tarleton.

Today our second and third parallels were outflanked by the rebels during the past night, as the rebels opened one of the bastions on their left.

This night the enemy delivered a strong cannon and musket fire, which we answered with only a few bombs from our Number 6.

The 8th - At daybreak the commanding general sent Major Crosbie into the city once again, informed General Lincoln that Fort Sullivan was in our hands, his cavalry was destroyed, our approaches were nearing his defenses, and there was no hope of his being reinforced; and ordered the fortress to surrender with the warning that if the obstinate defense continued, he would be responsible for the harsh treatment accorded his troops. Although General Lincoln admitted the truth of the situation and also knew his provisions were exhausted, he believed that his obstinacy would instill determination against our assault, which he hoped to defeat with the help of his numerous cannons, because our fleet could do nothing to assist. At that the French counsel, who did not wish to be taken prisoner, emphasized that it would take time to change the embrasures and to strengthen the defenses. This was another factor in the surrender negotiations. Other objections to General Clinton's capitulation articles were pointed out, so that the writing of these went back and forth until

The 9th - when everything fell apart at eight o'clock in the evening. Our batteries and those of the enemy cannonaded one another, mixed with platoon firing and the throwing of bombs throughout the night. The sky was filled with fire and it seemed to us as if the earth shook. General von Kospoth, in his headquarters at an hour's distance from the city, was injured by a cannonball which caused a pot hanging over his bed to fall on him.

However, our firing was as nothing compared to that of the enemy. It is customary during every siege in the world, that the firing of the besieging force must be stronger than that of the force being besieged, in order for the first to protect the works undertaken against the fortress. With us the opposite was the case, in that the besieged had five embrasures against each one of ours. Despite this great difference, we proceeded with our efforts, which were greatly aided by the loose, sandy soil, so swiftly that we extended our third parallel to the right against the enemy's left wing, all the way to the canal and laid out a new battery. The duty for the jaegers, who had to hold down the enemy's flanking batteries, was difficult and dangerous.

The 10th - The heavy cannonade continued causing the death and wounding of twenty men, including one jaeger. During the night we built a covered passageway across the canal and passed the first enemy abatis. A lodgment was also begun within thirty yards of the enemy abatis, although the enemy fired heavily with cannons and muskets against it.

The 11th - During our entrance into the trenches today we took a different route through a covered-over swamp. Nevertheless, we had to tolerate the cannonballs. The lodgment begun during the night could not be occupied yet but the work on it was continued. The rebels continued their cannonade and doubled their small arms fire, which latter made it necessary for me, as I had to support this new project, to place my thirty jaegers within twenty paces of a detached enemy position. Consequently the parallel was almost completely exposed to the enemy musket fire. I asked the English colonel commanding in the trenches to issue us ammunition from the Light Infantry supply, which we then fired so continuously that in two hours, from 2,000 rounds, almost none remained.

Meanwhile the general-in-chief gave the batteries the order at nine o'clock in the morning, as he was justifiably annoyed by the foolhardy resistance of the enemy commander, to fire on the city. Within a short time seven houses were set on fire. When they were in full flame, he halted the firing in order to give the hard-headed individual something else to think about. However, as the enemy continued to fire with cannons and muskets, our batteries began to fire shells into the city. Pressured by this fierce confrontation, at two o'clock in the afternoon, General Lincoln sent an adjutant, accompanied by a drummer, with a letter to the general-in-chief. Lincoln wished to give in to the suggested points, but requested that the militia and citizens of Charleston not be treated as prisoners of war. The general-in-chief refused this request and Lincoln was forced to surrender the city according to the articles which the general-in-chief thought appropriate.

Thereupon it was ordered by both sides to halt all hostile action. The conditions under which Charleston was surrendered are as follows:

- - - - - - -

[At this point Bartholomai lists the capitulation agreement signed by Lincoln, Clinton, and Arbuthnot on 11 May 1780 at Charleston. They are omitted from this translation, and the account resumes on 12 May.]

- - - - - - -

The 12th - At four o'clock in the afternoon, the garrison, consisting of between 4,000 and 5,000 men, marched out of the city, playing a Turkish march, and, as prisoners of war, stacked their weapons between the two abatis. One company of English and one company of Hessian grenadiers, with two cannons, occupied the defenses; the 7th, 42nd, and 63rd Regiments occupied the city; and the admiral occupied the works which covered the harbor.

Upon entering, a large English flag was raised over the city gate, which was saluted with 21 shots from the cannons in our positions.

All the siege troops moved out and formed two lines.

The rebels appeared thin, miserable, ragged, and very dirty. Their officers appeared to be primarily young people and poorly dressed, each in a different colored uniform and with different facings, which gave the officers of their army the appearance of comedians about to commence a show, which together with their troops, without shoes, made a very comical scene.[3]

Chagrin and anger, on the other hand, were to be seen in all their faces.

Among them were 7 generals, 26 colonels, 42 lieutenant colonels, 105 captains, and, including the militia and French, 6,000 men.

The names of the generals were as follows: Major General Lincoln, Brigadier General [Charles] Scott, [Daniel] Huger, [William] Woodford, [William] Moultrie, [Lachlan] McIntosh, and the French engineer, [Louis le Begue de Presle] Duportail.

The troops consisted of the following brigades:

Colonel [Bernard] Beekman's Artillery Brigade: 1) Continental Battalion 2) Independent Company 3) Charleston Battalion 4) Cannoneers 5) Smith's Carolina Continental Battalion.

Colonel [Maurice] Simon's Charleston Brigade: 1) Colonel Schmid's 1st Battalion 2) Colonel Ager's 2nd Battalion 3) Monsieur Britigney's Corps.

Brigadier General Scott's Brigade: 1) Colonel Marion's South Carolinians 2) Colonel Thompson's South Carolinians 3) Colonel [Archibald] Lytle's North Carolinians 4) Colonel Hopkin's Virginians 5) Colonel Schmid's Virginians.

Brigadier General Huger's Brigade: 1) Colonel Clark's North Carolinians 2) Colonel Patten's North Carolinians 3) Colonel [Robert] Mebane's North Carolinians.

Brigadier General Woodford's Brigade: 1) Colonel Russell's Virginians 2) Colonel Gist's Virginians 3) Colonel Nevil's Virginians 4) Lauren's Light Infantry.

Brigadier General McIntosh's Militia Brigade: 1) Colonel Maybank's 2) Colonel Garden's 3) Colonel Shivin's 4) Colonel McDougal's 5) Colonel Giles' 6) Colonel Hicks' 7) Colonel Richardson's 8) Colonel Kirshaus' 9) Colonel Goodwyn's 10) Colonel Harlington's 11) Colonel Tinning's.

General Lincoln's adjutant, who was dressed completely in a liver-colored summer suit, wore a wide green sash across his body, which indicated he was the adjutant general.

We captured fifteen flags, 343 cannons, including 21 metal ones, and 2 mortars, as well as several howitzers and coehorns, and 5,416 muskets, mostly of French and Portuguese manufacture. The best muskets and flints, for the most part, had been thrown in the water.

In addition to those items, we captured large magazines of rum, rice, and indigo, as well as a large amount of munitions.

We took a total of 49 ships and 120 boats of various kinds, among which were the frigate *Boston*, now the *Charleston*, of 36 guns; *Providence*, 32 guns; *Ranger*, now the *Halifax*, of 24 guns; and *Avanturier*, 24 guns, as well as *Pulakko*, 18 guns; and five three-masted ships. Nine ships were sunk, including an old East Indiaman ship of 50 guns; the frigate *Queen of France*, 32 guns; and three three-masted ships. In the Wando River, thirteen vessels, including one with three masts, loaded with cargo, fell into the hands of Lord Cornwallis' Corps.

The 13th - During the afternoon the captive officers, of whom there were a great many in the city, gathered improperly and loudly shouted, "Congress lives!" As an uprising was feared, their sidearms were taken from those gentlemen.

After the capture of this strong and in many respects, for English weapons, exceptionally important city had been successfully accomplished, the following commendation was published for all the troops, today:

Headquarters, Williams' House
Charleston, 13 May 1780

The commanding general is obliged to praise the army, which through its bravery and hard work earned the right to capture this important place He takes an inexpressable pleasure in extending his thankfulness in the fullest manner.

His Excellence is fully obliged to General Lord Cornwallis, Major Generals Leslie, von Huyn, and von Kospoth, and Brigadier General Paterson for their dedication to duty during the siege.

All the artillery officers, British as well as Hessian, the officers of the Jaeger Detachment; Captain Elphinstone, as well as the naval officers and seamen, who served on land, at all times have His Excellence's greatest respect for their conduct in support of all operations.

His Excellence also must thank Colonel Webster and his corps which cut off the enemy's main line of communication.

Especially thanked are Colonel Tarleton and the Cavalry and Infantry of the Legion, which enabled them to have so much success over the enemy.

The commanding general is indebted to Major Ferguson for his devotion to duty and especially to his demonstrated knowledge of field fortifications.

To Major Moncrief, however, who developed the plan for this siege and carried it out with such good judgment, tireless effort, and bravery, and to the capable officers serving under him and every other person in the department, who deserve unlimited thanks, His Excellence wishes he could find words to more fully express his highest praise.

The 14th - We were employed taking over magazines and other items. I went into the city and found the following to be worthy of note:

The city of Charleston lies at 32^{0} 30' north latitude, is built at the end of the neck between the Cooper and Ashley Rivers, and is a bit more than a mile long and a good half-mile wide. It consisted of about 800 houses, because many have burned during the disturbances of the present war, and not yet rebuilt. There are no suburbs. However, there are a number of houses built near the gate and along the defenses which, because they are separated from the rest by a space of about fifty to sixty yards, give the appearance of a suburb.

When entering from the land side, the city does not present a pleasant sight, either, because in this region most of the houses are only one story, built of wood, and none has any external improvements. However, farther into the city and pleasantly located on the water front, two and three story houses are to be found which are built of brick and decorated with various types of artistic pillars. Almost every house has a garden which is tastefully laid out and tended with much care. It is a shame that most of them are in ruins, because during the siege the inhabitants dug trenches which were then covered over with sand and boards. They lived in those holes where they felt more secure from our bombs than in their houses.

The streets are wide and laid out in a regular manner but not paved, which makes walking in the deep sand and the great heat very difficult. There are many beautiful churches in the city, one of which has an excellent organ.

I have seen graveyards which at night, in the warm climate, did not give the appearance of such. What the remaining houses lack in outward beauty was offset by the inner splendor and cleanliness. A German count would not be ashamed to live in the house of an ordinary citizen of Charleston. Large mirrors, beautiful tapestry, and mahogany furniture, very artisticly made, are the usual decorations.

The reason for this splendor, and above all the great riches of the inhabitants, is the advantageous position of the city for trade, provided by the Cooper and Ashley Rivers and the creeks which enter them and on which the products of Georgia and North and South Carolina can enter and exit the harbor.

The inhabitants, except for the native born, consist primarily of German, French, and Spanish. Their religion is a mixture and not of great importance to the residents, who, in addition to their wives, are served by Negroes and Mulatoes, and lead a life style similar to that of a Turk. Also, Christians, Jews, and Quakers intermarry. The most respected citizens have fled and those who remain here, in part from fear, in part from spite, have hidden underground.

Annoyance and anger are seen in every face. Above all, they can not stand the sight of the jaegers, which is natural, because they all served under arms and according to reports of their officers and all captured letters, the jaegers and the bombs caused the majority of casualties, so we can not expect any special kindness.

What Charleston's defenses consisted of, were as follows:

On the land side - a regular hornwork with eighteen cannons, which is called the old royal defenses. The scarp is a wall of brick which is covered with oyster shells and a cement coating two feet thick, which therefore does excellent service because it can not be breached by the largest cannons, but only gives way, and also a swampy ditch spanned by a stone bridge.

The gate which is in the middle of the revetment is protected by a lunette filled with earth, which has a double palisaded trench. Under the covering fire of small arms from that position is an entrenched position in the form of a half-moon, opened toward the city, which has a trench six feet wide and equally as deep, between a double row of palisades, sheltered behind a strong abatis. The entrance to that position is also through a half-moon with a trench covered by a movable *chevaux de frise*. On both flanks of those positions, two detached positions have already been laid out, protected by small arms fire, of which the one on the right rests against the Cooper River and the one on the left on the Ashley River. Both are covered to the rear by two other trenches. The entire front of the positions is protected by a swamp which has an ebb and flood tide from the two rivers. Through that flooded area there had been a twelve feet wide and six feet deep canal, running 100 yards in front of the trenches, to carry the water, by means of dams, past the swamp to the trenches. It too was behind an abatis over which a portable bridge had been constructed and the entrance through the abatis had a well-guarded swinging gate. The detached defenses were connected with the main entrenchment by palisades and trenches and, during the siege, by a revetment. It was planned to have those on the left connected in the same manner, but they were too close and therefore the left wing was the weakest point.

Therefore, if an enemy captured those detached works, the rest of the defenses could be attacked in the rear.

The French engineer Duportail, who had been sent here fourteen days before the capitulation by General Washington, discovered the weakness of the detached positions and therefore included the hornwork in the system of trenches. If we had not completed our work so swiftly, he would have been able to put the defenses in a much better condition.

On the water side - the defenses which covered the wharves and the harbor were laid out very well and provided with revetments, especially the so-called royal position, which was built of brick and oyster shells, also. The eighteen feet thick breastwork consisted of whole palmetto logs, through which, as previously noted, no cannonball can penetrate. They were filled with packed sand. At the point of the neck lay a fort which, like the point, formed a triangle. It was built with traverses of the same material and had three tiers of cannons, consisting of twenty-seven 18- and 24-pounders, which completely covered the harbor. Therefore the only way that the city could be attacked from the water side was with floating batteries or bomb galleys. The Cooper River was blockaded with sunken ships, except for a narrow channel, which was covered by the small arms fire from the defenses. On the Ashley River side were all the wharves from which it could be anticipated that his batteries could not be adequately fired upon through the logs, and furthermore, the defenses contained 100 or more cannons. For these reasons it was impossible to attack the city with ships from the water side. If a landing with flatboats were to be tried, the entrance to the channel leading to the city was so narrow that it would have been necessary to tolerate a dangerous cannonade. If even this were to be risked, the troops going ashore would still be sacrificed needlessly, because of the narrow defiles.

The 15th - During the afternoon a great misfortune struck Charleston due to the carelessness of the English. The artillerists were occupied taking weapons of the captives into a building, which had been an enemy magazine, when it blew up.

Six buildings, including a poorhouse and a brothel were destroyed in the flames, and, not counting the many residents and rebels, 200 or more of our men were lost, including the English artillery Captain

Collins, a Hessian artillery officer, Lieutenant McCloy of the 42nd Regiment, seventeen English and two Hessian artillerymen, a Hessian grenadier, and many English and Scottish soldiers. Without describing the sad sight of shattered, maimed, and half-dead people, who were struck down at the same time, or by the discharge of 5,000 mostly loaded weapons, many who were at a great distance were killed and wounded, and all the swords of the captured officers were melted. As great as this misfortune was, it could have been worse as another magazine containing 400 barrels of powder was located only 200 yards away. If this had caught fire a quarter of the city would have been laid in ashes, as in the vicinity of the magazine there are only wooden houses.

There are two reasons for the catastrophe. Either a loaded musket must have fired when it was thrown in and had ignited the stored powder, or a rebel had intentionally set it off in anger. Neither is an excuse for the English carelessness. What reasonable person would thoughtlessly throw loaded weapons into a powder magazine when a struck flint, resulting from a fall against another weapon, could cause the weapon to fire?

And if it were set, why wasn't such a dangerous place better guarded, and why was everyone allowed to enter? If this misfortune will instill greater vigilance remains doubtful, as there was another powder magazine on the Cooper river which was provided with a sentry who paid little heed to persons entering. This was very disturbing to a conscientious Hessian officer, until he was able to convince the English officer to keep a better guard on it in the future.

If this unfortunate event had not occurred, this long, complicated, and difficult siege, which was conducted with a few cannons against the enemy's numerous weapons, would have cost only a little over 200 men, because the rifle fire of the jaegers, which must have seemed incredible to a European, was employed daily against the enemy cannons in order to silence them. Therefore the enemy, behind his strong defenses, lost more than 600 men. In order to maintain strict law and order in the city, the Ditfurth and Huyn Regiments marched in to reinforce the garrison.

The 16th - Work began on removing the cannons from our lines and the fleet came up to the city through the widened channel.

The 17th - Work commenced on the preparation of the necessary passes so that the enemy militia could be sent home until their exchange.

The 18th - Today all the Negroes and horses were brought together to begin covering our trenches.

The 19th - The cannons were taken aboard ship, the city defenses cleaned, and demolition of our trenches was continued as swiftly as possible.

The 20th - In order to reduce the threat of a secret uprising, the captive officers were sent to Haddrell's Point under escort, from which place their parole allows them to travel within a radius of six miles.

The 21st - As it was recalled, that the rebels had hidden many magazines inland, the Light Infantry and Queen's Rangers marched at daybreak today toward Dorchester and Strawberry to seize them.

The army, except for the Charleston garrison, received orders to prepare for embarkation.

News was received from Lord Cornwallis that as soon as his corps had arrived at Manigault, the rebels had abandoned Georgetown and retreated toward Camden. Many residents of South Carolina came to us with their horses and weapons in order to fight for the royal army.

The 22nd - As the Jaegers and Grenadiers, in part because of the long, hard sea voyage, in part because of the half-rotten rations and the extremely miserable muddy water drawn from the swamps and filled with many insects, had lost their health and strength, their baggage was sent to Charleston today. To avoid the heat of the sun, the Jaegers, the English Grenadiers, and three battalions of Hessian grenadiers marched to Ashley Ferry and halted at evening in the woods.

The 23rd - Early in the morning we moved on to Ashley River and set up a pleasant camp close to the river. The healthy air and the so long-desired fresh water were both new experiences for us. As the Ashley River, because of the swampy banks, nurtured many types of vermin, we had all kinds of snakes in the vicinity of our camps. The Negroes were asked why these dangerous animals, which often came on land, were not killed off, and received this answer. The favorite food of the crocodiles was dogs and wolves. As there were a great many of the latter in this region, and because of the grazing land, the cattle were rounded up in the fall by the inhabitants. Therefore, these animals would be attacked by the wolves if the crocodiles were killed off. But the wolves did not remain in this area where there were crocodiles.

The 24th - We undertook a patrol today to get fresh meat for the troops.

The 25th and 26th - We remained quietly in place. There are a great many beautiful white cattle here. The local beef and veal was not good to eat as it tasted like skunk-cabbage, which the cattle here frequently eat.

The 27th - Our corps, under General von Kospoth, marched back into our former camp outside Charleston. On the way we found a young crocodile about an ell and one-half in length. This animal is almost identical in form to a lizard.

The 28th - Colonel Abercromby also returned with the Light Infantry and entered his former camp. The French merchants, who since the rebellion had gathered in Charleston, were told to sell their merchandise within three days and to leave the city. Some officers and men from the garrison, who had been released on parole but then joined the rebels, were caught by Lord Cornwallis' troops and put in jail.

The 29th - The transport ships loaded provisions and fresh water and then lay at anchor at the wharf.

The 30th - The Jaegers went aboard the transport ships *Apollo* and *Dispatch*.

The 31st - The Hessian and English Grenadiers went aboard ship. Our daily provisions were very difficult to obtain because, despite the general-in-chief's order that all stores were to be opened on 1 June or he would forcibly open them, there was still nothing to buy from this stubborn nation.

June 1780

The 1st - The following was published in orders for the army:

Having learned that a troop of rebels was on the border of South Carolina, Colonel Tarleton was ordered to go there by Lord Cornwallis. At three o'clock in the afternoon on 29 May, after having traveled 105 miles in 54 hours with the cavalry and the infantry of the Legion, with the latter mounted behind the cavalry soldiers, the detachment met the rebels, consisting of the 11th Virginia Regiment, several detachments of other Virginia regiments, and some artillery and cavalry, under the command of Colonel [Abraham] Buford, near Waxhaws, on the border between North and South Carolina. Tarleton called on them to surrender according to the same terms under which the Charleston garrison had surrendered. This was absolutely refused. Therefore the action began in a woods. Because of the necessity of leaving some horses behind and because he had to post a large number in reserve, the colonel could not attack with his full command. Therefore he took only 270 men, cavalry and infantry, but because he allowed the cavalry to use sabers and the infantry to charge with bayonets, he was able to rout the enemy. One lieutenant colonel, three captains, one adjutant, one quartermaster, and 97 privates were killed. Three captains, five lieutenants, and 42 men were wounded, and two captains, one lieutenant, and fifty men were captured. Only a few saved themselves by flight. Three standards, two 6-pounders, two royals, two wagons with ammunition, and 26 wagons with weapons and equipment were captured. Our losses consisted of two officers and eight privates killed, one officer and fourteen privates from the infantry and three officers and thirty men from the cavalry wounded.

The 2nd - This morning the Queen's Rangers went aboard ship. The warships and frigates assigned to escort our fleet set sail, passed through the channel, and dropped anchor with the fleet near Sullivan's Island.

As Charleston must be adequately occupied and in order to take the rest of South Carolina from the rebels, as well as to insure that this newly acquired province will not be attacked by the enemy, Lord Cornwallis remains as governor and general-in-chief in South Carolina with the following troops:

General Prevost commanded the Wissenbach and D'Angelleli Regiments, as well as the militia, which constitute the occupation force for Savannah, where a secure citadel was established so that the garrison could be reduced. However, as the general returned to England, Colonel Clarke assumed command.

At Charleston where General Paterson commanded, the 7th, 63rd, and 64th English Regiments and the Ditfurth and Huyn Hessian Regiments were the garrison.

In addition to those forces, General Cornwallis retained:

Two light infantry companies from the 71st Regiment, one from the 60th Regiment, and one from the 16th Regiment.

Two grenadier companies from the 71st Regiment, one from the 60th Regiment, and one from the 16th Regiment.

The 23rd, 33rd, and 71 English Regiments, Brown's Corps, York Volunteer, North and South Carolina Volunteers, North and South Carolina militia, Ferguson's Corps, a detachment of York Provincials, and the mounted and foot members of the Legion, three troops of the 17th Dragoon Regiment, the Savannah Light Horse, a corps of artillery and pioneers, and Lord Rawdon's Corps.

The Engineer Major Moncrief took over the task of repairing and improving the Charleston defenses.

The 3rd and 4th - The remaining troops went aboard their assigned transport ships, which then met a provisions fleet coming from New York.

This was the end of an expedition, which drove the French commitment out of its defenses, completely removed its presence, and nearly eliminated all Congress' credit, which is most necessary for independence. And, if this seems to be an exaggeration, it can still be shown that:

1) We suppressed the rebellion in South Carolina

2) Retained Georgia

3) Secured a firm foothold for the reconquest of North Carolina and other provinces, and

4) The rebels were forced to divide their forces, so that we were able to send reinforcements quickly, by sea, which because of the great distance offset the rebels quick movement on land.

\- - - - - - -

Notes

To Preface and Introduction

1. British Museum Additional Manuscript 21813, f. 33, 3 June 1776.

2, Bernhard A. Uhlendorf (trans. and ed.). *The Siege of Charleston, With an Account of the Province of South Carolina; Diaries and Letters of Hessian Officers from the von Jungkenn Papers in the William L. Clements Library* (Ann Arbor, 1938), 13.

3. British Museum Additional Manuscript 23649, f 17, 10 February 1777; 21813, f. 54, 29 March 1779.

4. Erhard Staedtler. *Die Ansbach-Bayreuther Truppen im Amerikanischen Unabhaengigkeitrskrieg, 1777-1783* (Erlangen, Germany, 1955), 98.

5. *Ibid.*,96.

To the "List of Officers"

1. I do not understand why Feilitzsch list the "Illustrious Jaeger Corps" and the "Illustrious Field Jaeger Regiment" separately but listed some of the same names under both headings. Possibly the first listing represents those initially sent to America, although I have never seen the commandant, von Schilling-Constadt, nor Major Pickelshieim listed as being in America.

2. Until May/June 1778 the 1st or Ansbach Regiment was called the Eyb Regiment, as indicated under Feilitzsch's entry of 7 March 1777. After Colonel von Eyb returned to Europe, Colonel Voit von Salzburg assumed command and the regiment became the Voit Regiment.

3. Or Seiz.

4. Or Ellrodt.

5. The 2nd or Bayreuth Regiment was initially called the Voit Regiment. After May/June 1778 when Colonel von Voit assumed command of the 1st Regiment, the 2nd Regiment was designated as the von Seybothen Regiment. It was never the Eyb Regiment.

6. Or Metzsch.

7. Or Ciriacy.

8. Originally only one company of Ansbach-Bayreuth jaegers went to America in 1777. Other companies were sent out during the following years until finally the six companies in America were organized as a jaeger regiment.

Diaries of two Ansbach Jaegers

To 1777 (Feilitzsch Diary)

1. A member of the Ansbach Regiment wrote a diary entry that the mutiny was started by the Bayreuth Regiment, and a member of the Bayreuth Regiment wrote a diary entry that the mutiny was started by the Ansbach Regiment. As Feilitzsch was not involved as a mutineer, his account is probably confirmation that the mutiny started in the Bayreuth Regiment. Johann Ernst Prechtel. *A Hessian Officer's Diary of the American Revolution* (Bowie, MD, 1994), 283; Johann Conrad Doehla. *A Hessian Diary of the American Revolution* (Norman, OK, 1990), 10 March 1777.

2. Pottigheim in the German text.

3. The Count of Hanau, the ruler of Hesse-Hanau, was also the Hereditary Prince of Hesse-Cassel.

4. Feilitzsch sometimes uses the German measurements of an hour which equals about two and one-half English miles, and German miles which equal six English miles. I have translated all measurements to the English equivalents unless specifically noted otherwise.

5. Possibly due to the animosity between the jaegers and the infantry regiments, as a result of the jaegers having fired on the infantry at Ochsenfurt, the jaegers traveled to the Dutch port at a distance and time behind the infantry.

6. Other ships assigned for the use of the Ansbach-Bayreuth forces were: *Stag, Friendship, Symetry, Durand, Myrtle, Hopewell, Diana,* and *Providence (2)*. Public Record Office 5/140, f. 91.

7. The Jaeger Company, "the Finest Body of Men I ever saw", according to a return of 19 February 1777, had the following organization: 1 captain, 1 1st lieutenant, 2 2nd lieutenants, 2 sergeants, 1 quartermaster sergeant, 1 Surgeon's mate, 5 corporals, 1 tent attendant, and 87 privates for a total of 101 men. The infantry had taken the oath at Nijmegen on 25 March 1777. Charles Rainsford. "Commissary Rainsford's Journal of Transactions, Etc., 1776-1778", *New York Historical Society Collections, XII* (New York, 1879) 357 and 407; Prechtel, *A Hessian Officer's Diary*, 25 March 1777.

8. Another account of this incident is that Peter lowered himself on a rope into the sea. *Ibid*, 18 May 1777.

9. Feilitzsch and some of the other Hessian diarists called the American provinces, islands.

10. Feilitzsch apparently spelled most American names phonetically. Tustin's research for the Ewald diary (see the Preface of this volume) made identification of place names quite simple for me.

11. As seen in the diary entries the Ansbach-Bayreuth Jaeger Company was integrated with the Hesse-Cassel Jaeger Corps when it reached America.

12. This is apparently a reference to a Hesse-Cassel jaeger.

13. The officer was Captain Johann Ewald of the Hesse-Cassel Jaeger Corps, who was cheated out of the prize money which the fleet represented. Johann Ewald. *Diary of the American War* (New London, 1979), 76.

14. This probably should be Gooch's Mill. The other places have not been identified.

15. 2nd Lieutenant Carl von Forstner.

16. This was the Battle of Brandywine.

17. This was the English night attack against General Anthony Wayne at Paoli.

18. This was the Battle of Germantown.

19. This was the unsuccessful Hessian attack on Red Bank.

20. This would have been Fort Mifflin on Mud Island.

21. This probably should be Darby.

To 1778 (Feilitzsch Diary)

1. In this case the host was probably the owner of the house who had to accept English or Hessian officers as paying guests.

2. Feilitzsch indicates here that American soldiers would desert to the English side, join a loyalist unit, get new uniforms, and then desert back to the American army.

3. This sounds like the description of a robin.

4. Possibly this should be Dorchester Road.

5. These little marks in the German text, here and later, may be due to gaps in the writing of the original diary or may indicate portions which the copyist could not decipher.

6. This is the first of several references to Indians fighting for the colonists.

7. They sailed to New York.

8. A large number of prisoners were exchanged during this period.

9. Feilitzsch gives the name as Euriston; Tustin as Eayrestown, Earystown, Aristown, and Irestown. Ewald, *Diary*, 403.

10. This was the Battle of Monmouth.

11. Vlaatisland may be Block Island. The units were on their way to Rhode Island from New York.

12. The reader will notice later that Feilitzsch found fault not only with Americans, Philadelphia, and New York; he did not like Holland nor the Dutch, nor even Cologne.

13. The 'in German' is inserted by Feilitzsch as he used the German equivalent of Spitting Devil.

14. This is Bruchings in the German text.

15. This was Lieutenant Wilhelm Joseph Juliat who had deserted from the Hesse-Cassel Landgraf Regiment at Rhode Island. Ewald, *Diary*, 153 and 407.

16. An extract of the Bartholomai diary follows in this volume.

17. Apparently Long Island Sound.

To 1779 (Feilitzsch Diary)

1. This would seem to be Major Prueschenck.

2. This entry was obviously not copied in its entirety as there seems to be a possible reference to a chain obstruction across the river missing in the German text.

3. Again, a portion of the text seems to have been omitted.

4. Samuel River in the German text.

5. Possibly "Be alive!" or some such precautionary alert notification.

To 1780 (Feilitzsch Diary)

1. Words within the quotes are in English in the German text.

2. Words within the quotes are in English in the German text.

3. I have not found an equivalent measure for a 'Stang'.

4. Words within the quotes are in English in the German text.

5. Words within the quotes are in French in the German text.

6. This date, which is partially missing in the German text, may be either the 13th or the 15th.

7. Cramon was senior to Feilitzsch and assumed command of the transport returning to Ansbach-Bayreuth.

8. Rore Ruhre in the German text.

To the Bartholomai Diary

1. This was the fleet which took Feilitzsch back to Europe.

2. This unit was formed in accordance with an order issued at New York on 8 December 1779: "From the following listed regiments, a detachment of chasseurs is to be taken consisting of three officers, eleven non-commissioned officers, two drummers, and 100 men. From

1) The Leib Regiment - one non-commissioned officer and nine privates.

2) The Landgraf Regiment - the same.

3) The Hereditary Prince Regiment - one officer, one non-commissioned officer, one drummer, and nine privates.

4) The Prince Charles Regiment - one officers, one non-commissioned officer, and ten privates.

5) The von Ditfurth Regiment - one non-commissioned officer and ten privates.

6) The von Donop Regiment - one non-commissioned officer and eight privates.

7) The von Lossberg Regiment - one non-commissioned officer and six privates.

8) The von Mirbach Regiment - one non-commissioned officer and eight privates.

9) The von Bose Regiment - one non-commissioned officer and nine privates.

10) The von Huyn Regiment - one officer, one non-commissioned officer, one drummer, and eleven privates.

11) The von Buenau Regiment - one non-commissioned officer and eleven privates.

TOTAL: three officers, eleven non-commissioned officers, two drummers, and 100 privates.

Second Lieutenant [Ernst Wilhelm] von Anderson, of the Hereditary Prince Regiment, whose date of rank is 26 February 1776, and who previously served with the chasseurs, is ordered to do so again. The other two officers, second lieutenants, one each from the Prince Charles Regiment and the von Huyn Regiment, have more recent dates of rank. For the soldiers, dependable and robust men from Hesse are to be chosen and no foreigners, and as many as possible are to be taken from those who served in the chasseur corps previously." "Order Book of the Illustrious von Mirbach Regiment, from 10 March 1777 to 28 June 1780", a German manuscript in the

Lidgerwood Collection of the Morristown National Historical Park, Morristown, NJ, translated by Bruce E. Burgoyne.

3) Although Bartholomai thought the Americans made a comical scene marching without shoes, Berthold Koch, sergeant in the von Bose Regiment, noted three days after the 16 March 1781 Battle of Guildford Courthouse, "However, the situation was now very bad for us. We had won, but we had no foodstuffs, no shoes on our feet, and no shirts on our bodies.... It was decided to begin the return march to the sea." Berthold Koch. "An Electoral Hessen Infantryman ... in the American War of Independence", edited by Hans M. Braver, *Zeitschrift fuer Heereskunde* (Berlin, 1932) translated by Bruce E. Burgoyne.

INDEX

----, Peter 7
ABERCROMBY, Col 120 127 153 Lt Col 123 Robert 95
ACKERMANN, Nick 13
ADAMSON, John 96
AGER, Col 146
ALTENSTEIN, Heinrich 2
ALTHOUSE, 98 John 95
ARBUTHNOT, 145 Adm 69 131 136 137 142 Marriot 64 94 Vice Adm 95
ARMAND, 66 Charles Tuffin 62
ARNIM, Gen 28
ARNOLD, Friedrich Sigismund 3
ASHE, Lovett 142 Lt 143
ASHLEY, William 116
BABCOCK, 67
BACH, Joseph 3
BARTHOLOMAI, 145 Christian Friedrich 3 49
BECK, Johann 53
BEEKMAN, Bernard 145
BICKEL, Alexander Wilhelm 60 Lt 62
BODUNGEN, Capt 141
BRITIGNEY, Monsieur 146
BROWN, 155
BUFORD, Abraham 154
BURGER, Surgeon's Mate 70
BURGOYNE, 59 62 John 24
BUSCH, Ehrenfried Hannes Friedrich Ferdinand 3
BUTLER, John 52 65
BYRON, 64 Adm 63 John 55
CAITHNESS, Earl Of 125
CAMPBELL, Archibald 53 Capt 117
CATHCART, Lord 95
CHISHOLM, 109
CLARK, Col 146
CLARKE, 114 115 116 118 119 120 Alured 108 Col 123 155
CLINTON, 145 Gen 40 45 95 107 132 143 Henry 39 86 93
COLLIER, George 65
COLLINS, Capt 150 151 Robert 130
COLUMBUS, Christopher 103
CORNELIUS, Lt 58 Maximillian 56
CORNWALLIS, 46 Capt 114 Charles 20 91 Gen 27 28 29 41 62 155 Lord 95 96 108 113 116 119 120 123 128 137 138 141 142 146 147 152 153 154
CORTLANDT, 56
CRAMON, Capt 81 82
CROSBIE, Maj 132 143
D'ESTAING, Charles Hector 55 92 Comte 63 93 94 95
DAIG, Johann Georg 2
DEAHNA, Justus Hermann 3
DORIS, 67
DRAYTON, 118 122 123
DUNDAS, Thomas 120
DUPORTAIL, 150 Louis Le Begue De Presle 145
EBENAUER, Friedrich 1 31 Lt 56
ELPHINSTONE, Capt 123 147
EMMERICH, 45 46 48 63 Andreas 53
ERB, Georg Christoph Elias 3 Johann Philipp 2
EVANS, Henry Francis 128

EWALD, Capt 40 56 102 104 116 121 124 128 Johann 9 96
FEDER, Friedrich 1
FEILITZSCH, see VONFEILITZSCH
FENWICK, 109 120
FERGUSON, 56 95 110 133 155 Maj 147 Patrick 48
FONTAS, Col 120
FRANK, Albert Magnus 3
FREUENHAGEN, Lt 26
FRISCH, Johannes Paul 3
FULLER, Benjamin 123
GARDEN, Col 146
GELIAT, 48
GIBBE, 111 113 125 127 128 131
GILES, Col 146
GIST, Col 146
GOODWYN, Col 146
GRANT, Gen 53 James 52
GRAY, Charles 20 Gen 46
GREY, Gen 28
HAMILTON, 114 119 John 122
HAMMOND, 46 120
HANGER, George 95
HARLINGTON, Col 146
HAUSSELT, Johann Leonhard 3
HEINRICH, Johannes 24
HENRY, John 102
HERRNBAUER, Johann Friedrich 2
HICKS, Col 146
HINRICHS, Capt 106 120 123 136 140 Johann 96
HOPKIN, Col 146
HOWE, 96 Gen 12 19 39 Lord 44 Richard 11 97 William 10
HUDSON, 119 120 121 124
HUGER, Brigadier Gen 146 Daniel 145
HUYN, Gen 113 121
INDIAN, King Of The Lower Creeks 135
JOHNSON, Henry 61
KING, Of England 6 135 Of The Lower Creek Indians 135
KIRSHAUS, Col 146
KLING, Jacob Ernst 96 Jakob Ernst 3
KNYPHAUSEN, Gen 41 46
LAFAYETTE, Maria Joseph Marquis De 38
LAUREN, 146
LESLIE, Alexander 40 95 Gen 111 116 120 122 123 Maj Gen 147
LETHUSCH, 119
LIEBERMANN, Johann Adam 70
LINCOLN, Benjamin 92 Gen 94 111 113 130 132 135 143 144 146 Maj Gen 145
LINDEMEYER, Hermann 2
LINNING, 121 124 129
LOAN, 120
LOREY, Capt 56 58 Friedrich Heinrich 42
LUTZ, 31
LYTLE, Archibald 146
MAITLAND, Col 112 John 111
MARION, Col 146
MATHEW, Edward 55
MAYBANK, Col 146
MCCLOY, Lt 151
MCDOUGAL, Col 146
MCINTOSH, Brigadier Gen 146 Lachlan 145 William 135
MEBANE, Robert 146
MECAN, Thomas 121
MIDDLETON, 122
MODEL, Johann Heinrich Hartmann 2
MONCRIEF, 126 James 92 Maj 111 125 127 132 147 155
MONIZEN, 66
MONTLUISANT, Lt 53
MORG, Christian Caspar 3
MORRIS, 69 96
MOULTRIE, William 145
NAGLER, Georg Friedrich Sigismund 2
NASH, Lt 118
NEVIL, Col 146
OTTO, Christian Philipp 3
PATERSON, 129 Brigadier Gen 147 Gen 108 110 111 121 122 123 124 137 155 James 95

PATTEN, Col 146
PFLUG, Andreas Friedrich 2 70
PFROMEL, 35
PHILIPSE, 43 46 56 59 62 64 67
PRECHTEL, Johann Ernst 1
PREVOST, 62 Augustine 55 91 Gen 59 61 92 104 154
PRUESCHENCK, Maj 56
PULASKI, 110 113 115 118 120 133 Casimir 48 92
RACK, 122
RAPP, Friedrich Jakob 2
RAWDON, Lord 155
RICHARDSON, Col 146
ROBERTSON, 56
ROBINSON, 61
RODNEY, George 77
ROSE, 120 122 Tom 119
RUMMEL, Johann Jakob Conrad 2
RUSSEL, Col 146
RUTLEDGE, Edward 141
SAVAGE, 120
SCHAEFFER, Lt 11
SCHEFFER, Johann 96 Lt 118
SCHMID, Col 146
SCOTT, 119 121 Brigadier Gen 146 Charles 145
SEIDEL, Johann Christoph 2
SHIVIN, Col 146
SIMMONS, 109
SIMON, Maurice 146
SMITH, 145
STIRLING, Thomas 54
STRAHLENDORF, Lt 77
TARLETON, 143 Banastre 95 Col 124 133 134 142 147 154
THOMPSON, Col 146
TINNING, Col 146
TONKEN, Capt 103 104 108 123 Thomas 101
TRAILLE, Peter 95
TRITSCHLER-FALKENSTEIN, Ernst 1
TRYON, Gen 60 62 William 54 91
VAUGHAN, Gen 60 John 56
VERNIER, Pierre Francois 133
VONADELSHEIM, Carl Friedrich 2
VONBARTHOLOMAI, C F 86
VONBEUST, Ernst Friedrich Carl 2 Philipp Otto Heinrich 2
VONBIBERSTEIN, Wilhelm Friedrich Marschall 1
VONBODUNGEN, Franz Christian 37 96
VONBUBNAANDLITITZ, Franz 3
VONCRAMON, Capt 23 36 43 Christoph Gustav 12
VONCYRIATZY, Andreas Gottleib 2
VONDERHEYDTE, Moritz Wilhelm 1 3
VONDIEMAR, Julius 7 Justus 1 3 Wilhelm 2
VONDONOP, Carl Emil Ulrich 9 Col 23 24 Karl Moritz 46
VONELLROD, Christian Philipp 1
VONEYB, Col 2 36 37 Friedrich Adolf Carl 3 Friedrich Ludwig 2
VONFALKENSTEIN, Carl Christian Ernst Tritscher 3
VONFEILITSCH, Heinrich Carl Philipp 1
VONFORSTNER, Lt 22
VONGNIESENAU, August Wilhelm Neidhardt 3
VONGUETTENBERG, Georg Friedrich Philipp 1
VONHELLER, Ferdinand 3
VONHUYN, Gen 108 Johann Christoph 95 Maj Gen 147
VONKELLER, Friedrich 1
VONKNYPHAUSEN, Wilhelm 18 96
VONKOENITZ, August Christian 1 August Christian Friedrich 3
VONKOSPOTH, Gen 123 143 153 Heinrich Julius 95 Maj Gen 108 147
VONKRUSE, Wilhelm Friedrich 2
VONLINSING, Otto Christian Wilhelm 127
VONMASSENBACH, Julius 3
VONMETSCH, Friedrich Christoph Heinrich 2

VONMOLITOR, Christian Theodor 2
VONPICKELSHEIM, Diedrich Ernst Georg Spiegel 1
VONPRUESCHENCK, Ernst Karl 47
VONQUESNOY, Georg Heinrich 2
VONREITZENSTEIN, Christoph Ludwig Rudolph 1 Edward 84 Friedrich Ernst 3 49 Friedrich Wilhelm 1 3 Lt 66 Ludwig Heinrich 2 S T Christoph Ludwig Rudolph 3
VONROEDER, Friedrich Wilhelm 1
VONSALZBURG, Christian Ernst Voit 1 Friedrich August Valentin Voit 1
VONSCHILLING-CONSTADT, Franz Carl Georg 1
VONSCHOENFELD, Carl Friedrich Rudolph 1 3
VONSCHONAUER, Wilhelm 66
VONSEITZ, Friedrich Philipp 1
VONSEYBOTHEN, Col 2 Franz Johann Heinrich Wilhelm Christian 2
VONSICHART, Johann Friedrich 37
VONSTEINZUMRECHTENSTEIN, Heinrich Carl 1
VONSTRAHLENDORF, Adolf Daniel 70 Adolph Daniel 2
VONSTREIT, Maximilian 2
VONTEUFSTETTIN, Albert Ernst Ludwig Trechsel 2
VONTUNDERFELD, Georg Gustav Lebrecht 2
VONVOIT, Col 1
VONWALDENFELS, Capt 43 Christian Ernst 1 Christoph Friedrich Joseph 3 42 Joseph Christian Friedrich 1
VONWANGENHEIM, Capt 66 Friedrich A J 11
VONWEITERESHAUSEN, Carl Alexander 1
VONWESTERHAGEN, Max 137
VONWINZINGERODE, Lt 136
VONWREDE, Capt 22 47 Carl August 11 See Also Wrede Remove Page Twenty Three 23
VONWURMB, Ernst Wilhelm Friedrich Adolph 3 Maj 123 128 140 Philipp 96
WAGNER, Johann Conrad 2 Johann Emanuel 24
WALDENFELS, Capt 56
WASHINGTON, 42 94 130 Col 122 124 133 142 Gen 92 111 150 George 34 91 Lady 46 121 William 120
WATT, Abraham 111
WEBSTER, 114 122 129 133 Col 110 115 116 118 120 123 125 134 136 137 147 James 108 Lt Col 127 132
WEINHARDT, Heinrich 2
WEISS, Head Forester 84
WHITE, Col 142
WIEDERHOLD, Johann Heinrich 83
WILLIAMS, 147
WILSON, 109 111 113 125
WINZINGERODE, Johann Ernst 96 Lt 104
WOLFF, Johann Heinrich 58
WOLFFEN, 71
WOODFORD, Brigadier Gen 146 William 145
WREDE, 23 Capt 26 31 See Also Vonwrede 26
YORKE, John 95